D1226935

THE END OF A ROAD

By the same author

The Dead Sea Scrolls
The Sacred Mushroom and the Cross

JOHN M. ALLEGRO

The End of a Road

The Dial Press  New York 1971

Originally published in England
by MacGibbon and Kee, Ltd.

Library of Congress Catalog Card Number: 77-145179

Printed in the United States of America
First printing

CONTENTS

PREFACE

THIS book is a companion volume to my recent study on the origins of Christianity, *The Sacred Mushroom and the Cross.* From the first philological discoveries on which the prime thesis of that work is based, it became evident to me that their repercussions must spread far beyond the relationship between the Semitic and Indo-European languages, and the underlying meanings of biblical mythologies. The Bible, for good or ill, has become for hundreds of millions of people throughout the world a source of religious revelation. From it Jews, Christians and Muslims have sought to discover facts about the nature of God and his will for the world, even the way they should conduct their lives and personal relationships. In these exegetical endeavours, their priests and prophets have been largely undeterred by the patent fact that no one has really known much about the nature and origins of Yahwism or Christianity, being unable to decipher with any certainty the name of the god or the patriarchal heroes of biblical stories. Nevertheless a vast body of historical and theological speculation has been built up over the centuries on the basis of these obscure Semitic and Greek writings. Younger scholars too often find that researches which do not start from these 'established' positions are suspect and even, in some institutions of learning, virtually impossible.

Being myself in the happier position of teaching in a university well known for the liberality of its outlook, and owing no allegiance to any religion, I was able to work freely in this highly controversial field, pursuing the results of the philological and mythological discoveries outlined in *The Sacred Mushroom and the Cross.* Although I tried to restrict my discussion in that book to those aspects of my researches which bore directly upon the nature and purpose of the biblical writings, particularly the New Testament, I could not help but be aware that the results must have implications far outside the literary field. For example, the fertility origins of the Hebrew god Yahweh, and the sex-drug nature of the mystery cult underlying 'Christianity', were so contrary to popular supposition about these religions that the credibility and authority of 'orthodox' Jewish and Christian teachings, not to say teachers, must inevitably be brought into doubt. Lay people might with reason suspect that for more than two thousand years the world has been subjected to doctrinal propaganda about the Bible, rather than objective interpretation of its words, and that its ecclesiastical teachers had been more concerned with indoctrinating certain theological propositions than laying bare its original meaning. Such questionings may lead to the conclusion that professional exegetes of the Bible have set out deliberately to deceive the laity.

This would be a harsh judgement. Most biblical expounders have not been Semitic or Greek scholars themselves but pious men and women for whom the Scriptures have served as a source of inspiration for theological speculation. In most cases, their religious hypotheses were not formed from any logical reasoning based upon biblical 'proof', but had been accepted as true on the authority of their spiritual mentors and Bible texts secondarily adduced as confirmation. The original propounders of these theological truths had themselves sought inspiration more from a mystical intercourse with their god than a rational, historical study of ancient literature. Nevertheless, there must have been a time in the development of Judaism and Christianity when their leaders resolved upon ridding their cults of embarrassing features inherited from an earlier age, as in the Old Testament when, under the kings Hezekiah and Josiah, relics of the old fertility beliefs and rituals were rooted out of Yahwism and denounced as contrary to the real nature of the cult. Today we know better: Yahweh was himself a fertility deity, whose worship by real or simulated sexual intercourse and related rituals was an original part of the cult. Whatever justification the religious reformers of these and later times may have claimed for their conscious manipulation of the ancient traditions, there must have been some point in their deliberations where they agreed to deface the past and start anew. They took what they believed to be the essentials of their Faith, discredited any practice or belief which conflicted with their ideas and promulgated their refined code as the original religion revealed by their god, claiming that over the course of time it had become perverted through man's sin. Certain myths handed down over the centuries and relating directly to the old fertility-drug cults were 'historicized', and a theology made to hang upon the actions and words of their legendary characters as real people. The Jewish 'Exodus-Sinai' myth became thus actual history, belief in every word of which was made obligatory on the faithful, as the 'Jesus crucified' story was within a generation or so of its devising made for Christians a central feature of God's redemptive activity in man's history.

It is easy, looking back, to condemn these decisions to re-direct the thinking of their followers as, at the least, ill-conceived, even as cynical 'brain-washing' of superstitious and ignorant believers. But one has first to remember that the division that we in the western world draw between fact and fiction was not then, and still is not today, in those parts of the world, so pronounced. Myth and history were confused, and in a religious context, virtually inseparable. If they had not been, one cannot imagine, for instance, how intelligent men could have for so long refused to believe that the world was not a flat dish surrounded by water and, until even more recently, that its creation had not occurred only some six thousand years ago and that the whole human race could not be traced back to two persons in Mesopotamia named Adam and Eve.

The fault lies not so much in the men responsible for promulgating what we now see to have been false ideas, as in the nature of religion itself. The believer claims that he can communicate with his god through prayer and revelation in a way denied to non-religious people, and therefore has a source of information not subject to the usual control of rational criticism. He 'believes' in his deity and miracles not because they can be proved to exist or to have happened but because his mind has been conditioned by his faith to receptiveness. He is 'inspired' rather than intellectually convinced. He tests the truth of any proposition not by its inherent probability but by the nature of the authority that presents it, and its part in the religious Faith to which he has submitted his will and intellect.

What we might call 'tampering with the truth' for the sake of inducing an assent to doctrines about a god and his will for mankind is probably harmless enough while they relate only to religion proper, that is, the mystical relationship between the worshipper and his deity. Trouble starts where that religion promotes ideas about day-to-day conduct, political or moral. Thus, fired with emotion for a completely irrational policy, as for instance, that which inspired such uprisings as devastated Judaism in the first and second centuries, the believers can be too easily persuaded into acts of madness against the wellbeing of the community. On a less dramatic scale, a religion which prescribes for its adherents certain moral attitudes, however rational and beneficent, can too easily bring them into disrepute if it is later shown to be based on a fallacy or serious misconception. The danger is then, of course, that 'the baby is thrown out with the bath water'; something tested by experience and found to be good will tend to be rejected with an irrational belief no longer tenable on quite other grounds.

This is the situation which now threatens our western civilization. Some parts of the accepted morality of what we call 'the

Christian way of life' have been tied to a particular religious cult. Unhappily, that faith has made historical claims about its reputed Founder, Jesus, which were never sufficiently substantiated by external evidence for the weight of doctrine they were made to carry. Today we know this story to have been quite imaginary, and its composition and transmission devised for an esoteric purpose connected with the secret nature of the cult. At the time of its inception the real nature of the Jesus legend must have been well known, certainly among its originators and, as we can show, even among Jews outside the cult for some considerable time afterwards. But 'orthodox' belief came to insist upon the myth's historicity, and those who disagreed, including presumably those who knew the truth and wished to preserve it at least among the initiates of the secret society, were driven out into the wilderness.

Now, in the twentieth century, we are faced with a situation when the old moral sanctions, already under criticism for their inadequacy before new problems posed by our technological society, are suddenly cut adrift from their religious moorings. The original religion of 'Christianity' none but a drug addict would today wish to pursue, and however worthy some of the moral tenets expressed in the New Testament may still be, we can hardly be expected to accord them any more than a pragmatic authority. If it works in modern society, well and good; if not, throw it out with the rest of the discredited cult of the sacred mushroom.

In one way, as I suggest in this book, this 'clearing of the decks' could not have come at a better time; if we are going to be able to tackle realistically new problems about life and death and the rights of the individual in an ever more closely integrated society, we are better viewing them afresh without any dogmatic preconceptions handed down as the inspired word of a Jewish or Christian god. Even those of the 'Ten Commandments' that had any ethical relevance at all were never very satisfactory guides to the resolving of particular moral problems. Each needed further elaboration and application to specific situations, and it was in this rubric that the real guidance lay. General principles are fine so long as they do not come in the way of practical decision-making.

Perhaps a more urgent problem posed by the breakdown of credibility in the Jewish and Christian Faiths, is the reliance placed upon their assurances about a loving, personal God who never fails His people in times of personal distress. It is difficult to feel the same trust in a deity originally conceived of as a mighty penis in the sky, ejaculating semen as rain. Later theologians may have propounded more sophisticated notions about their god, but traces of belief in the old fertility Yahweh/Jehovah, the spermatozoa deity, are still discernible in the Old Testament and reappear in the mystery religions of the sacred fungus, which came down in certain underground sects of Judaism and 'Christianity'. Furthermore, the Church has focused the adoration of its faithful onto the incarnated God, Jesus, as a more comprehensible concept for ordinary men and women than the formless, ethereal Life-force of sophisticated theology. If this 'Jesus' is now shown to have no more material substance than a mushroom, how shall the pious worshipper find comfort in his adoration?

Whatever worthy motives led Jewish theologians and Church fathers to propound myth as history and command intellectual allegiance to these doctrines from their followers, it is difficult not to feel contempt for people who have thus brought unnecessary suffering upon millions of simple folk who trusted their spiritual mentors too well. In their daily lives believers have looked to the spiritual presence of the Jesus they have been taught to worship, believing that any suffering they may have to endure cannot compare with that which their Lord himself had known on earth; whatever temptation to sin they might be called to resist, he too had faced and been victorious; whatever heartache a son might cause his mother, she could feel no greater anguish than the virgin Mother who watched her Son suffer on the cross. Now they have to be told that their Lord was a mushroom, his mother a fungus volva, and his heavenly Father a mighty penis in the sky.

Some may ask if they have to be told. Should scholarship however well-founded and objective in conception and execution be allowed to upset a faith which brings comfort to so many millions? No one working in the field of biblical studies has not at some time faced this issue, or had it forced upon his attention. We all know that there is a great gulf between modern, so-called 'liberal' biblical scholarship and the man in the street, or pew. The doubts a clerical scholar may freely voice in his seminary concerning the historicity of scriptural traditions will rarely be heard from that man's pulpit on a Sunday. To hear some well-known biblical scholar talk on radio or television at Christmas or Easter, one might never guess for a moment that he and most of his ecclesiastical colleagues have long ago surrendered to the realm of fiction most of the New Testament stories relating to the birth of the Christ child at Bethlehem or to his subsequent death on Calvary.

This is not to accuse these worthy men of downright dishonesty and blatant falsification of the truth. There are well recognized ways of discussing such subjects in public which seem to imply no dissent from the popular, uncritical view of the historicity of the New Testament narratives. But careful examination of these seasonal exhortations will show that at the same time they do not commit the speaker to a positive commitment to the conventional viewpoint. Some might call the procedure 'double-talk', as indeed it is, but the justification of such equivocation would be that since no one knows all the answers to all the problems posed by the biblical records, it is better to leave the layman with the generally accepted view rather than that he should have his simple faith upset by every will-o'-the-wisp theory or speculation that comes out of the specialists' debates.

We heard this viewpoint expressed frequently in the last decade or so concerning the Dead Sea Scrolls. Unsuspected caches of ancient manuscripts were discovered in 1947 and thereafter in caves near the Dead Sea in Jordan. They were written mainly in Semitic and were generally believed to have come from a Jewish sect called the Essenes who were previously known only from the reports of ancient historians like the first century Josephus. It had long been suggested that this group, from the little that was known about their beliefs and way of life, may have been the 'missing link' between orthodox Judaism and Christianity. If true, this would, of course, tend to diminish the uniqueness of the latter Faith and the authority of its Founder. Now that we had at last first-hand accounts of Essenism from the sect's own library, speculation ran high that we should discover the truth of the theory and lay bare perhaps the Essenic nature of Christianity. Such has not proved the case in just the straightforward way at first envisaged. For one thing, face-to-face comparisons between the Semitic Scrolls and the Greek New Testament are not satisfactory. The secondary Christian traditions have first to be translated back into their presumed Semitic form, which allows of no certainty since we lack any original Semitic accounts of the words and actions of Jesus. In the second place, if, as the ancient writers maintain, the Essenes were a closed society, requiring a strict probation of their neophytes before admission to the inner circle and their most closely guarded doctrines, it is hardly likely that such secrets would be committed to parchment and left in caves for anybody to find and read. In other words, Essenism still remained a mystery, quite as deep and unrevealed as the origins of Christianity. We had enough to show that there did exist an overall similarity between the two sects, and indeed, scholars have found many instances where the New Testament Greek reflects the same Semitic phrase as appears in the Scrolls. There are points of contact in their attitude to the prophetic books of the Old Testament and in their manner of interpreting Scripture. But real progress in drawing out lines of connection depended upon our ability to work far below the local level of immediate contacts between the Scrolls and the New Testament; we had to discover their common denominator in a mystery cult which had its origins in earliest Yahwism, and long before that in the oldest strata of Near Eastern religion. This has now been possible, as readers of *The Sacred Mushroom and the Cross* will know.

But at the time when speculation was most rife on the significance of the Dead Sea Scrolls for uncovering the beginnings of Christianity, there was heard abroad the querulous voice of the clergy, largely caught off balance by the discoveries and questions about the Jewish background of their Faith with which few had even bothered to concern themselves, demanding that their laity be not 'upset' by theories which could not and probably would never be proved. We heard much of the 'dear old soul down the road' who was apparently much disturbed by these reports of a second Jesus, or a previous 'Sermon on the Mount', and was utterly at a loss to know whom to believe. Let us all maintain a discreet silence, these voices from the cloisters urged, and if and when the problems posed by the Scrolls are solved, then we can speak with one voice and authority. In any case, they went on, nothing that has been found or can be found will ever upset the Faith, for Truth belongs to the Church.

In the days when the parson was really as ignorant as his layman about the historical background of the biblical writings and their purport, this unwillingness to rock the doctrinal boat without certain evidence had something to justify it. But when, a century or so ago, biblical scholarship shook itself free from the chains of orthodoxy and streaked ahead, leaving conventional interpretations and old notions about verbal inspiration far behind, there arose a new situation. Now the informed cleric did not speak from ignorance; he was aware that he could no longer subscribe to naïve ideas about the Bible traditions such as his laity still held. He was also aware that his professional future lay in their hands, so he was obliged to ease his way equivocally round the subject, or content himself with vague generalities about God's revelation of truth being geared to man's ability to receive it, which left his hearers a free hand to believe or not to believe as they judged themselves inspired by God to apprehend truth.

Unhappily, the Church left the unsatisfactory state of affairs too long, and events overtook whatever plans she may have had for bringing her laity up to date with modern scholarship. The discovery of the Scrolls and their likely impact on modern research into Christian origins was widely publicized. Almost overnight the man in the pew was made aware of trends of modern thinking and the possibilities that had long been posited for the lines through which Christianity may have emerged out of Judaism. What the simple believer had been traditionally taught to believe was a sudden, unique and sparklingly fresh revelation about God through His Son, Jesus, superseding at a stroke the old Jewish dispensation, was, he now discovered, being regarded by his mentors as a natural development from the old order, owing more to the deliberations of the Church's first theologians than any new, once-for-all proposition by a uniquely inspired god-man.

Books and pamphlets then began to appear by the hundred trying, as their largely clerical authors explained, to put the discoveries into perspective, and almost all ending with a chapter assuring the believer that nothing had happened which need upset his faith. But it was too late. Their faith had been upset, not so much in the validity of Christian teaching and the authenticity of the New Testament (few, any way, could understand what all the fuss was about since the Scrolls do not mention Jesus), but in their clergy, who had now started, often for the first time, to talk the language of the seminary in the pulpit. Furthermore, the more intelligent layman was beginning to ask the sort of questions the academics had been vainly asking for decades, and realizing that there was no satisfactory answer to be found, at least within the framework of accepted Christian dogma. He began to appreciate just how sparse is the evidence not only for the New Testament traditions about Jesus and his death, let alone the 'miracles', but for the history of the Church in those crucial first decades. The phrase 'Gospel truth' began to take on a hollow sound.

Thus, those few of us working within the Scrolls field who owe no allegiance to any religious body, could hardly take seriously the accusation that we were upsetting the faith of the simple believer. The Church itself, by its own paltering with the truth at the very beginning of its history and more recently in its deliberate double-talking, had betrayed the trust of its flock. We who are commissioned by State-financed centres of learning to discover truth without fear or favour cannot be expected to withhold our findings from the general public until such times as the clergy have had the opportunity of bringing themselves and their laity up to date with modern research. The material I have mainly used to make the discoveries outlined in *The Sacred Mushroom and the Cross* has been available to Christian scholars for the past hundred years. They chose to gloss over the difficulties in the supposed 'Aramaic' words and phrases in the New Testament which do not make sense at all or do not fit their 'translations'. Bound originally by the dogma that every word of the Bible was inspired directly by God and thus incontrovertible, how could they dare to challenge their validity? Starting from the assumption that the Israelites were Semites and their religion was Semitic, how could they reasonably question the Semitic origin of the divine name Yahweh, revealed to His Chosen People in the deserts of Sinai? Even after the discovery of ancient Sumer and its literature in the middle of the last century, the decipherment of the divine and patriarchal names in that medium was not seriously attempted. How could a Semitic religion inspire a pre-Semitic mythology? And without an historical Moses, what becomes of the whole Exodus story, and the redemptive theology on which it was based?

It is pointless now, however, to apportion blame for the anguish of mind that must beset the Christian world in the loss of its supposed Founder from history, and in the reduction of his career and death to the life-story of a mushroom. This book is not a post-mortem examination of a moribund Church. In it I am not primarily concerned with the cult of the sacred fungus, which fully deserved all the abusive epithets heaped upon its perversions by the Romans when they tried to suppress the 'Christians'. It deals with the end of one road, and more particularly the opening up of a new, wider highway for all men to travel. We shall look to some of the problems now facing mankind and bearing down on us with the dramatic advances in modern technology in a shrinking world, and see how old and inadequate moral sanctions can be revised or replaced by new ones. We shall discuss how the present catastrophe of a discredited Christianity can be turned to good account through seizing the opportunity for fresh creative thinking in a society freed from the inhibitions of religious dogma. Let the dead bury their dead.

THE END OF A ROAD

CHAPTER ONE

The One God

RELIGION is the relationship between a man and his god. It is born out of his sense of weakness and frustration in the face of a largely hostile environment. The extent to which religion dominates a man's life depends therefore upon his self-confidence. Flushed with the success of his own efforts, man needs no master but himself. Dispirited by failure, or the blows of fortune, he looks to his god for comfort and hope of future restoration. Even when things went well, when his granaries were full, his cisterns flowing with water, his stockyards and rivers teeming with life, early man was beset with fears for the future, lest in the next year drought or plague strike his land. He plied his god with praise and bribes for the continuance of his good fortune, and tried to lure the deity into remaining with him for all time. He built fine houses for the god, and employed representatives to enact continual rites of appeasement and stimulation to promote his procreative activity.

For the god was life. The oldest god-names known from the Near East relate to his creative power. He was thought of as a mighty penis in the skies, ejaculating semen in the violence of the storm, and thereby fructifying the womb of mother Earth beneath. The Greek Zeus and the Hebrew Yahweh (Jehovah) derive from a common linguistic source, and both mean spermatozoa, 'seed of life'. Embedded within both names is an ancient Sumerian word, symbolized by the single letter 'U' meaning 'fertility', perhaps the most significant phoneme in the whole of human speech. 'U' was the name of the old Sumerian storm-god; when he spoke, it was the shriek of the wind, the scream of ecstasy at the height of the divine orgasm. 'U' was the liquid that spurted from the lips of the swollen glans and bore divine life to earth. 'U' was the copulatory act itself, the bestriding of a woman by her mate, the mounting of beasts or, more remotely, the fecundation from above of the vaginal furrows of the earth by the god. 'U' meant 'to have mastery over', to be lord and husband. It signified the sensual, savage world of sexual domination and fructification. It lay at the heart of ancient religion.

The culture of ancient Sumer was not the first; man had been an intelligent being for hundreds of thousands of years before the people we call Sumerians first set foot in Mesopotamia. But for our Graeco-Semitic civilization their culture was the beginning; it is from their language, as now for the first time we can recognize, that our own ultimately derived. It is from their ideas about God that ours came, transmitted through the religious writings of the Jews and Greeks. Yahweh, Zeus and Allah are one: all mean 'the sperm of heaven'.

It was the Sumerian culture that, about 3500 BC, invented writing, and made communication of ideas and thus history possible. Before then, paintings daubed on walls, figurines crudely fashioned from clay, and the like, offer modern enquirers our only ancient evidence for the religious questing of primitive man. With writing, first crudely incised picture diagrams on clay tablets, later stylized symbols and finally alphabets, man could transmit commands, accounts and then stories, songs and liturgies over distances of space and time. As early as 2000 BC Sumerian tablets were recording whole epics and cosmologies that had doubtless been transmitted by word of mouth for hundreds or thousands of years before that. The 'U' culture of Sumer was already old at the beginning of history.

If we want to know how and where Christianity began,

where its roots lay and how its philosophies were derived, we have to look not merely to the immediate hinterland of the Jewish Old Testament and the inter-testamental literature of the Apocrypha and the Dead Sea Scrolls, but raise our eyes to the very horizons of history. The 'Jesus' cult began long before that, but historically we first glimpse its essential features in the Sumerian 'U' culture, in the throbbing phallus of the Sumerian storm god. The name 'Jesus/Joshua' (the Greek and Hebrew forms) means 'the semen that heals' or 'fructifies', the god-juice that gives life. To be smeared with this powerful liquid, above all to absorb it into his body, was to bring the worshipper of the 'Jesus' into living communion with God, indeed, to make him divine. Thus was religion perfected, God and man made one, and the power of all-knowledge transmitted from heaven to mortals. In the words of the New Testament writer, 'you have been anointed by the Holy One and know all things' (I John 2[20]).

To the ancient, knowledge and fertility derived from the same source. The slimy juice that dribbled from a man's penis at ejaculation was a kind of 'spittle' in the old vocabulary. The organ was 'speaking' at the moment of release. In the grosser and more violent imagery of the storm, the divine phallus spat its juice into the wind and men saw it beating down on to the open furrows of the ground and sinking away into the terrestrial womb. They called it 'the Word of God'. To assimilate this Word into oneself was to have divine knowledge and thus power. The 'strong' man of a community, it was soon realized, was not the brawny fellow, much as he might boast of his prowess with an axe, a sword, a plough or his wife; it was the wise, the cunning man, full of arts and crafts, the seducer of his fellow-men and women. It was he who became rich at the expense of the labourer; it was he who survived the long hot summers of drought and watched lesser men gasp out their lives round dried up water-holes. He eked out his water ration from his cistern, hewn out of the rock whilst the fool had watched the precious fluid stream away down the wadi beds. That kind of wisdom was as god-given as the rain itself; to achieve it was to become, like the eaters of Eden's fruit, 'like one of us', the gods. Above all, the wise man knew the divine secrets of the herbs and their powers. He was aware that some plants and trees contained more of the god's sperm in their sap than others. There were herbs that could kill, and others that could heal. There were a few very special herbs, like the Mandrake, which could do both. To use this 'Holy Plant' safely, it was not sufficient to know where to find it; one also had to know when it might be picked, the time of day, the state of the weather. One had to know its secret names and recite them at the moment of plucking and at its administering. One had to know its antidote and the precise amounts of each, given in accordance with the previously determined susceptibilities of the 'patient'.

The wisest men of the community, then, were the doctors and the priests, and their store of herbal knowledge was the most precious and closely guarded possession of the professions. Through it they wielded great power over their fellows. Even the king, the personal representative of the god in any one city, depended on their information, guidance and good will for the continuance and effectiveness of his office.

The intimate relationship between the god and his priests found practical expression in the religious ritual of the temple, the god's house. There seems to have been a common pattern of architecture for the temple throughout the ancient Near East. The names applied to its various parts show that it was conceived of as a womb, in the innermost part of which, the 'uterus', the god dwelt and performed his acts of creation for the benefit of his people. It was the seat of the divine Word, and thus the source of oracular information imparted to the priest as mouthpiece of the god.

An essential part of the god-man relationship in times of uncertainty and crisis was to share in the divine knowledge of what was to come. Man must soon have realized that what separated him from animals and gave him a certain measure of control of his environment was the ability to reason and look ahead. Prognostication was the mark of human wisdom and to those especially favoured by the god, this ability to peer into the future raised them in esteem into a superhuman category. Of such were the doctors, priests and prophets of the ancient world, recipients of the divine Word. In the Holy of Holies, or 'Oracle' of the Hebrew temple, the high priest met Yahweh once a year and became, on behalf of his people, mystically endued with the god's holiness. He prepared himself by dressing up as the god, that is as the phallus, his headgear representing the glans penis and his body smeared with the saps and resins of those sacred plants deemed especially endowed with the god's semen. He became thus a 'christ' or 'anointed one', dripping with seminal fluid like the male organ in the vagina. His entry into the temple through the labial 'porch', past the hymenal 'veil' into the vaginal 'hall' and thus, on this special occasion, into the uterine 'Oracle' or 'Holy of Holies', symbolized the copulatory act of divine and animal creation. It was the hieratic equivalent of the imitative and stimulative act of the farmer copulating with his wife in the field after harvest, urging the god to fructify the ground afresh as the man impregnated the woman's womb. In the Christian Church today, the priestly processional from porch to altar, preceded by the cross, symbol of the conjoined penis and volva, culminating in the raising aloft of the Host, is but a traditional reflection of this age-old fertility ritual.

The prophet's relationship with the god was even more direct and intimate. By long preparation of his body and mind, by the subjection of his carnal desires, by fasting and abuse of his flesh, and particularly by the careful use of drugs, he could induce within himself a hallucinatory state which he explained as direct communion with God. Day-to-day objects and people about him seemed larger and colours more intense. He saw strange visions and heard voices deriving, we would say, from his own subconscious, but for him and the credulous onlookers, from the seventh heaven of divine perception. It was at such fleeting moments that man was permitted to glimpse the throne of God and even to carry back to the human planes of existence the so-called 'knowledge of God'. At that one glorious moment of revelation, the prophet became a participant in the divine mysteries; suddenly he knew by no normal means of rationalization or deduction the secrets of the universe and the purpose of life. And if the words he babbled at the time seemed to those about him the ravings of a madman, for those who believed that their hero had seen God, their very incomprehensibility seemed added proof of divine origin.

From such oracular babbling the prophet himself, restored to rationality, or more usually his intimates who had assisted him through the mystic veil, derived by imaginative ingenuity the answers to problems needing an insight into the future for their solution: Shall we go to war? Where are my lost asses? Will my son recover? and so on. However satisfied or disappointed the customers of such prophetic trafficking when the enemy stood at the gates, the asses remained lost, and the only son died, for the visionary himself the revelation remained unimpeachable. His fellow men, even his disciples, may have failed to understand, but for him who had seen God face to face, the vision remained. For that one moment he had become as God himself, knowing all things, having power over all things, seeing all things as they really are. No one could ever take away that experience, and the prophet's only desire was to repeat the process again and again; if possible, to remain in that sublime state of perception and never return to the shackles of the flesh, the cage from which he had found such blessed release.

The vision of the prophet in such moments of ecstasy was one of unity: one god, one purpose, one creative act and one stream of life. For mortals at the receiving end of creation, this conception of oneness was not immediately evident. Inanimate objects were different from living beings: stones from trees, a rotting carcase from a breathing animal quivering with life. Even among living creatures there were fundamental differences, like male and female, small and great, weak and strong. There were the great opposites of nature: heat and cold, light and darkness, sweet and bitter, and the fundamental composites of matter: earth, air, water and fire. But for the prophet in his moment of revelation there was an essential unity about the whole of creation, an harmonic beauty which defied adequate verbal expression. The greatest passages of Hebrew poetry attempt to express this organic unity and harmony of the heavenly world, helped to some extent by the peculiar genius of the language, but too often lost in translation.

In less elevated spheres of perception, the underlying unity of nature was not entirely lost upon the prophet's fellow men, however disparate in form and function natural phenomena appeared on the surface. The farmer recognized the need for a balance in his husbandry if the earth were to bear her fruit and his animals their young year after year. He knew as well as the modern agriculturist the need for leaving fields fallow after a time and the technique of crop rotation. Be over greedy and mother earth will take offence and deny her blessings. Deny fodder to your cows and they will refuse you milk. Overwork your ox and he will die under the yoke. Giving and taking are essential parts of the same creative process. To make demands without restoration is tyranny, whether of land, animals or subject peoples. The result is imbalance, barrenness of land and livestock, and political rebellion.

Perhaps only the religious mystic saw the unity of God sensually, but the ordinary man and the king knew its truth from practical experience. The social prophet translated this vision into no less tangible terms: if a man becomes rich at the expense of his neighbour and exercises his power over him at the expense of his human dignity, that underdog will turn on him. If a man denies another his natural rights, the god will restore the balance in this life or the next. If a man becomes prey to overweaning pride in his own efforts, the god will lay him low from his armoury of retribution against which man has no defence. The whole of what we call moral law was thus fundamentally an expression of the essential unity of the godhead and the associated balance of nature. In this sense, religion and ethics were inextricably related; sin was essentially an imbalance of the divine order. To commit sin was sacrilege.

For example, since spermatozoa was divine, to spill it wastefully, that is, to ejaculate it in a way that denied its proper function of fructification, was a sin against God. The balance of nature had been upset. The cycle of events that began with the man's own conception, his growth to maturity, his sexual stimulation and orgasm, was interrupted if he committed sodomy or buggery, or if he withdrew his penis from the vagina before ejaculation and, in the words of the story of Onan in the Old Testament, 'spoiled the semen on the ground' (Gen. 38[9]). As that miscreant was punished by a wrathful deity, so all who wasted the blessings of God, or in some way broke off the natural cycle by greed or laziness, laid themselves open to similar punishment. It is this basic moral law which underlies the Catholic Church strictures on birth control. Hence so-called 'safe period' copulation is, properly speaking, as 'sinful' as placing a rubber sheathing between the glans and the uterine cervix. Both methods of contraception are strictly 'unnatural' and god-denying.

Christianity, like all other religious manifestations of the Near

East, was derived ultimately from a fertility cult first seen in the culture of ancient Sumer. To grasp the fundamental principles of this nature religion it is insufficient to study the rituals by which religious ideas were expressed, or even to analyse the liturgies and functions of the temple cults. One has to probe to the meanings of the divine and cultic titles, and to see how these ideas expressed there were reflected in every aspect of ancient life. If God were life, then it is reasonable to assume all man's mortal experience was god-centred. There was no such thing as a Sunday evening religion. Man's relationship with the deity permeated everything he did: the food that he ate, the craft of his hands, the reasoning of his brain, his fears and hopes, his loves and hates. God was in everything, since he was the source of creation, and yet he remained apart and in control. He could give and he could withhold, bless and punish; his laws were immutable for man, but his actions could seem to mortal intelligence, at times quite arbitrary.

It was this uncertainty about God's will that kept man in perpetual subjection to his religious masters. Even when he obeyed all the rules he knew, preserved the balance of his taking and giving, made token reimbursements to the god of the first fruits of the harvest and the cattle-fold, yet disaster could inexplicably strike him or his household, and send him scurrying to the priest to know the nature of the sin he had unwittingly committed and the manner of its atonement.

If one could but have the knowledge of God, to eavesdrop on the councils of heaven, then man could better regulate his existence and avoid the pitfalls which beset him at every turn. If he knew there was to be a drought, he could store corn from the fruitful harvests. If he knew his land would be ravaged by an enemy, he might have moved away or harvested his crops and hid them before the onslaught. Above all, if he could learn the secrets of the herbs and taste the nectar of the god, the undiluted Word, he would know all things and for a moment at least shed his mortality and free his naked soul for the flight to heaven. Then, at last, he would find certainty, and freedom from fear.

Thus the fertility religion led to the mystery drug cults of classical antiquity and to its Christian manifestation. The 'flesh' and 'blood' that the Bacchic and Christian participant of the mysteries chewed and drank, so innocuously represented today in the Church's communion meal, was the 'Dionysus' and the 'Jesus Christ' by which he found salvation. The drug it contained offered spiritual release from the cloying sin that hindered the initiate's soul from complete absorption in the godhead. This was the ultimate mystery that the Church itself lost, consciously thrusting aside the essence of its potentially dangerous cult to achieve political accord with its temporal rulers.

Readers of *The Sacred Mushroom and the Cross* will know that the clues that led to the rediscovery of the particular drug source favoured by these mystery cults were primarily philological. The plant's identity was one of the most closely guarded secrets of the ancient world, so the pseudonyms by which it was commonly designated proliferated while the mystic names were known only to the favoured few. The breakthrough came when we discovered that the names of gods and plants which came down into Greek and Latin, the languages used by the classical botanists and mythmakers, like those of the ancient Semitic records, could be traced to a common source in Sumerian, the first written language of the world. We had thus a bridge between the old Indo-European cultures and the Semitic world which gave us our Old Testament and the ethnic source of the New Testament and Christianity. By re-examining these god and plant names in the Greek and Latin writings and breaking them down into their original Sumerian verbal elements, we found it was possible to retrace our steps on the other side of the bridge, so to speak, and lay bare the meanings and derivation of Hebrew god-names, and those of heroes like Moses and Joshua. So at last it has become possible to discover the real meanings behind the myths and legends of the Old Testament. Despite apparent differences in the language, background and details of the final forms of such myths, we can now begin to discern common themes in biblical and classical legends. The false division erected by the academicians between the Indo-European and Semitic worlds has gone for ever. The classicist must now be also a Semiticist; the Semiticist must feel equally at home in the classics. We can look forward to a new era in the study of ancient history and perhaps find fresh impetus for rediscovering common ground between East and West.

CHAPTER TWO

The Sacred Fungus

THE particular drug plant which our philological researches eventually isolated in the names and legends of the Bible was the red-topped mushroom, *Amanita muscaria* as modern mycologists call it. In its cap there lie several powerful drugs which give reactions varying between light euphoria to extreme physical violence and displays of almost supernatural strength. Characteristic of its effects are the hallucinations it gives its partaker, when objects are seen much larger than life (macroscopy) and colours more intense. Some users have reported having the illusion of travelling vast distances over space and time, floating free of their bodies, and enjoying unaccustomed spiritual perceptiveness. It is not difficult to find marked similarities between these effects of the Holy Plant, as it was called from the earliest times, with the prophetic experiences recorded in the Old Testament, and particularly in the psychological phenomena exhibited by such visionaries as Ezekiel. In the New Testament, similarly, we have at the beginning of the strange work called 'The Revelation to John' a clear portrayal of the red-capped *Amanita muscaria* seen under the macroscopic influence of its drugs:

> ... in the midst of the lampstands one like a son of man, clothed with a long robe and with a golden girdle round his breast; his head and his hair were white as white wool, white as snow, his eyes were like a flame of fire ... his face was like the sun shining in full strength (Rev 1[13-16]).

The reader will be well aware of the shape most recognized as characteristic of the mushroom or toadstool, to give it one of its very many folk-names. Above ground is the stem bearing on its top the umbrella-shaped canopy, or cap. *Amanita muscaria*'s most distinctive feature is the red canopy flecked with white spots or 'warts', and this fungus is the one most pictured in nursery storybooks as the home of elves and goblins. The 'warts' are in fact the broken fragments of the 'volva' or outer skin of the 'egg' from which it develops. Before its expansion, which can be extremely rapid, the fungus looks like a pigeon's egg half-buried in the soil, and indeed one of the oldest Semitic names given to the sacred mushroom was 'egg'. We can recognize the mushroom origin of a number of ancient myths by the relationship of the chief character to birds and their birth from eggs, as with Leda, Helen, and above all the Dioscuroi, the Heavenly Twins, Castor and Pollux. The Old Testament story of Jonah, whose name in Hebrew means 'dove', is also a mushroom tale, and it is this plant that fancifully gave the unfortunate prophet shade from the sun's rays as he sat outside Nineveh.

This volva or 'womb' from which the mushroom grows presented to the ancients one of the many puzzling features about the fungus. It appeared to be fertilized by no normal method; it had no seed and no root and, in fact, was a quite unique species of natural growth. The ancient folklorists concluded that the mushroom must be conceived by the direct action of God within the virgin womb. Since it appeared often after storms, they thought that the heavenly deity must have fertilized the virgin by his word in the thunder. The resultant baby mushroom, which grew into the shape of its divine father as a small erect penis, was thus in a special way a 'Son of God', and was called 'Son of Thunder'. The expression of these old fancies in the Virgin Mary and Immaculate Conception myth of the New Testament will be easily recognizable. The name 'Sons of Thunder' appears as a nickname given to two of Jesus's disciples, James and John, the so-called Boanerges brothers (Mark 3[17]). In the text, 'Sons of Thunder' appears as a translation of the strange and hitherto inexplicable 'Boanerges'. In fact, as is well known, if the latter word is Aramaic, a sister language of Hebrew and generally considered to have been the tongue used by Jesus, it did not mean 'Sons of Thunder'. Our new linguistic discoveries set forth in *The Sacred Mushroom and the Cross* have shown that 'Boanerges' is not Aramaic at all, but a Sumerian phrase descriptive of the mushroom. It portrays the fungus under the fanciful macroscopic guise of a man holding up the arch of heaven, a figure which finds frequent expression in ancient mythology, as in the legends of Atlas and Hercules. The phrase 'Sons of Thunder', therefore, is not a translation at all but an equivalent folklore name for the sacred mushroom.

This 'Boanerges-Sons of Thunder' combination is but one of several such ingenious disguises of ancient mushroom names in the text of the New Testament. An important and secret name of the fungus is transliterated into Greek letters and then given a pseudo-translation. To the cursory reader, and particularly to one for whom Aramaic was a foreign tongue, the 'translation' presupposed a Semitic original which could conceivably pass for the important cult word. Even when such apparent discrepancies have come in for intense philological study, the verdict has usually been that later scribes misread or misheard the original. Thus, for instance, 'Boanerges' was taken to be a mistake for something else meaning 'Sons of Thunder', or it is assumed that 'Boanerges' is right but unintelligible, and a later scribe hopefully added 'Sons of Thunder' as an ill-conceived attempt to explain the Lord's nickname for the hot-tempered brothers who at one time asked permission to call down fire on an unwelcoming Samaritan village (Luke 9[51ff]).

A similar instance occurs in the book of Acts when a disciple called Joseph is surnamed in the text 'Barnabas', and that name explained as meaning 'Son of Consolation' or 'Encouragement' (9^{36}). For centuries exegetes have been searching for a Semitic word which means 'encouragement' and looks like 'nabas' (the *bar-* element can legitimately mean 'son' in Aramaic), without success. Again opinion has usually resigned itself to assuming that a mistake has crept in, and that either the real name of the philanthropist is lost for ever, or a later commentator has added the 'translation' more out of piety than linguistic persuasion. As we can today appreciate for the first time, the name is not Aramaic or even Semitic, but is another ancient Sumerian descriptive title of the sacred fungus, and refers to the peculiar colouring of *Amanita muscaria*. The first element *bar-*, here as in other New Testament names, means 'skin' or 'container', 'pouch' or 'volva', its precise significance depending upon the context.

Perhaps most interestingly, this word appears in the surname of Simon Peter, 'Barjona', 'Bar-Jona' (Mat. 16^{17}). Usually assumed to mean 'son of Jona', it appears that this name is but a truer and more original form of an important name of the Holy Plant which has come otherwise down to us in the form 'Paeony', and has been applied to a very different species. In fact, the deep red crimson of the flower we recognize by that name is the distinguishing feature of the cap of the *Amanita muscaria* which, as we now know, has given original mushroom names to a number of words for red or crimson in Indo-European and Semitic. However, even as late as the time of the Roman naturalist Pliny the Elder (AD 23–79), there were stories told of the 'Paeony' which related more to the mysterious fungus than the innocent flower to which the name had become attached.

All the other names of the apostle, 'Peter', 'Cephas', even the unkind 'stumbling block' and 'Satan' (Mat. 16^{23}), relate to the mushroom, forming part of the rich store of its folk-nomenclature. Furthermore, this kind of false interpretation in the New

Testament is not confined to the proper names of its characters. Such well-known sayings as the words from the Cross, 'Eloi, eloi, lama sabachthani' (Mark 15^{34}), we have shown to represent one of the most important of the ancient names for the fungus. The difficulties which have always existed in the supposed translation, 'My God, my God, why hast thou forsaken me?' result not from a corrupt text as generally supposed, but from the purposely cryptic nature of the passage, indeed, of the whole book.

Even in those cases where no foreign word appears in translation on the surface of the Greek text, as in the Lord's Prayer, research has shown that its phrases are formed by word-play or punning on original mushroom names read as if they were Semitic words and then rendered into Greek. The opening invocation, 'Our Father who art in heaven' is nothing but a Greek version of an Aramaic phrase derived by word-play from an old name for the sacred fungus. It turns out that we have known it all along in the cabbalistic formula 'Abracadabra', which first appears in the writings of a second century Gnostic author. It was a magical phrase reckoned to have the power, if pronounced accurately and accompanied with various rituals, to drive out demons and heal diseases. The name Gnostic is given to a number of religious sects, of a pre-Christian origin but which manifest certain Christian terminology and ideas in ways that the Church considered grossly heretical. Gnosticism caused the Church much trouble in the first centuries, not least because its varieties of mystical experience and expression could not be controlled under one hierarchical authority and thus promulgated as the one, indivisible faith of the Church. Now that we are able to penetrate to the real fount of Christianity and the nature of its inspiration, the phenomena of Gnosticism can be reviewed and reassessed as very probably expressing some aspects of the cult more accurately than that which became the 'orthodox' faith.

In any case, its magical formula 'Abracadabra' came on down not only in our story-books but, as we see, in the disguised form of the opening words of the Lord's Prayer and elsewhere. It is an interesting thought that the invocation we teach our children to recite every day in their school assemblies is in fact a formula for exorcizing demons.

Now that we have at last begun to break the New Testament 'code', we can see how the Gospel narratives and teachings are based upon the age-old Jewish literary device of word-play or punning. What seems to us today to be a low form of wit was from the earliest times for the pious exegete a means of deriving from the sacred text of Scripture religious homilies and even 'history'. A synagogue teacher might stand before his fellow-worshippers, after the reading of the Bible, and begin to expound on the meaning of the text. When the face meaning had been adequately dealt with, he took the individual words and spun them out by splitting them into syllables, or relating them to similarly sounding words which, although radically quite unconnected, gave the preacher a link with some fresh elevating message for his listeners. Such performances found their merit in the value of the homiletic discourse and its persuasion towards the good life rather than in its philological expertise.

There are plenty of examples of this kind of word-play in the Old Testament, particularly in those stories woven around the birth and naming of the patriarchs, as we see in Genesis 29^{31} – 30^{13}. The modern Hebraist might well view the derivations there proposed for the proper names with dubiety, even astonishment, but the object of the author's efforts was not to teach his readers Hebrew but to demonstrate the relationship of the tribal ancestors of Israel to their progenitor Jacob, and to see in their names and circumstances of birth explanations for their subsequent histories.

The New Testament writers continued this literary tradition, but used it to weave a story of a hero figure Jesus who, after a short ministry in Palestine, fell foul of the machinations of Jewish leaders who coerced the Roman governor into putting him to death. By the same kind of word-play they spun out from well-known Old Testament texts, particularly those currently thought to foretell the coming of the Messiah or Christ, the stories of their hero. More importantly from their point of view, they wove into the narrative sayings and names formed by similar punning on the names of the sacred fungus.

The homiletics of the New Testament, despite the influence they have wielded through the Church, are not in general peculiar to Christianity; most can be found already in the Old Testament and contemporary Judaism. What is becoming clear is the way these moral exhortations have been framed to convey by word-play the secret names and incantatory phrases of the mushroom cult. Again the New Testament cryptographers are not breaking new ground in this literary device: close examination of the Old Testament 'Ten Words' or 'Commandments', shows that they have been verbally compiled on a similar basis, using certain very old names for the fungus. Indeed, the whole story of Moses ('the emergent snake' as his name may be understood), Mount Sinai, the two tablets on which the finger of God wrote the laws, and so on, are all part of mushroom mythology.

The essential truth of the Christian and Essene claims that they were the inheritors of the religion of ancient Israel may now be affirmed. The old Israelitish cult and mythology, the Yahweh-worship, the patriarchal legends, the sojourn in Egypt, and so on, are rooted in the religion of the sacred fungus, developed from the underlying fertility philosophy of the ancient Near East. Later Judaism purged itself of the old cult, then religiously unfashionable and politically dangerous, abandoned its secrets to small bodies of the faithful prepared to face persecution by the authorities, accepted the mythology as history, reoriented their theology around these 'acts of God' and came to terms with the secular powers. The same pattern was repeated with the Christians. The mushroom cult was driven even further underground, its adherents facing hideous tortures in the pursuit of their religious ideas, and there emerged an organization which accepted the historicity of their own myth, founded their Faith upon its hero as if he had really existed, and saw in his life, death and resurrection a crucial act of God in the history of mankind. This 'new Christianity' became not only socially acceptable, but part of the secular authority, and in due course its armies ruled a large part of the civilized world.

Of course, it has been long known that not all parts of the New Testament are to be taken at their face value. The book of Revelation has always been regarded as a cryptic and semi-political work concealing, for instance, the name of the hated enemy of the Christians, Rome, under the pseudonym 'Babylon'. The supposition must be that the book was expected to fall into the hands of the Romans and yet remain unrecognized for the violently subversive work it really was. What has not been hitherto appreciated, however, is that even the Gospels and Acts are cryptic documents. The discovery that proper names, incantations and the like have been given pseudo-translations expressly devised to deceive the casual reader, puts the lie to the whole story. It removes the main focus of interest in the writings from the innocent story of the good and pious rabbi, working miracles of healing and uttering statements about the nature of God and man and his religious and social responsibilities, to a hidden layer of meaning beneath the narrative and homilies. For if the writers are at such pains to conceal special names and incantations, then clearly these are of prime importance. When, on decipherment, they bear upon a mystery cult otherwise known to have existed for thousands of years throughout the ancient Near East, we must assume that the real affinities of Christianity lay in this secret religion rather than in the free-for-all evangelistic Gospel that is the purport of the 'cover story'.

If one had any doubts about the necessity for this secrecy about their cultic activities, one has only to read the accounts of the persecution of the Christian communities by their political masters. No words were too vile to use of the Christians, the worshippers of the 'Chrestus' as they are called. The tortures and degredations to which they were subjected if caught at their secret rites hardly bear contemplation. It was therefore vitally necessary to conceal the names of the sect's leaders, the places where they met and the secrets of the cult. It follows that even if there were in the first century a leader whom the sect venerated above his fellows, his name was certainly not Jesus/Joshua bar Joseph, his mother's name was not Mary, and his native village was not Nazareth, even if, indeed, there was at the time a Galilean village of that name. Furthermore, the administrative head of the cult was not called James, nor his successor Peter. The chief evangelist to the Gentile world was not called Paul, nor were the centres of the organization likely to have been the places named in Revelation as the homes of the 'seven churches of Asia' (1[4]), almost certainly a word-play for the seven stages of religious initiation. To have revealed in so open a fashion the names of personalities and places would have been sheer lunacy at a time when the 'Chrestus-worshippers' were being hauled from their cells, thrown to wild animals or crucified on burning crosses.

The kind of contempt shown by the Roman writers of the first and second century towards the Christians, in those very few places where they are mentioned at all, matches that displayed towards political rebels, particularly those fanatics who found in their religion the incentive to stir up trouble in the empire. Of such were the Jews of the First and Second Revolts of the first and second centuries AD, the so-called 'Zealots' and the followers of Simon Bar Kozebah or Kochebah. Our researches have shown a strong probability that the 'Zealots' at least were connected with the Christians as they were with the Essenes, and shared the same drug-cult that gave them hallucinations of a divinely ordained world domination.

In AD 70 the Zealot madness brought destruction upon Jerusalem and her temple. The Jews were dispersed from the city and thereabouts, and the cultic centre of Judaism was disrupted. The mushroom cult came under even fiercer attack and without the coordinating influence of the Jerusalem centre there was danger that its secrets would be lost. An important feature of the mysteries was the recitation of the names of the fungus and its demonic powers, the angels. It was essential that these ancient names and incantations should be repeated accurately. Of such were the secrets of the cult, normally transmitted only by word of mouth between priest and acolyte under strict oaths of silence. To the ancient, the name of the god was a powerful medium of influence; pronounced in the right way and accompanied with suitable mystic actions, all manner of magic might be performed. It had therefore to be reserved only for the god's servants, aware of the responsibilities such power carried with it. Normally in religious texts some surrogate for the name would be used, as we see in the Old Testament. Indeed, so rarely used was the secret name of the Israelite deity, that its proper pronunciation was lost entirely, for the Hebrew text preserves only the four consonants YHWH.

With the disruption of the cultic centre in AD 70 and the dispersal of the governing body of the Christian religion, it became essential to devise some means of coordinating belief and action and to maintain an accurate transmission of the sect's secrets by the written word. To write down such precious information involved fearful risks: not only that in the wrong hands could the power it offered be misused, even to nullify the cult's own influence over its members and other people, but its possession as an identifiable mark of a banned society would lay the recipient open to fearful retribution from the authorities. It is for this reason that no firsthand account of the classic mystery cults has come down to us. What little we know of their beliefs and practices is derived from the garbled accounts of witnesses outside the cult who would normally be barred from seeing the most guarded rites and hearing the most secret incantations. Just how garbled these accounts were, and how false and effective were the trails led by the initiates to mislead the outsiders, is only now becoming clear with the discovery of the cult of the sacred fungus.

It is ironic to think that this most looked-for of all ancient writings, a statement of beliefs and practices emanating from the heart of one of the most important mystery cults of the ancient world, has been in our hands for the past two millennia, unrecognized. The New Testament is, as now we can realize, the cryptically written aide-memoire of the mushroom worshippers. The 'Jesus', like the 'Dionysus' of the related Bacchic religion, is but a personification of the sacred fungus, the 'smeared' or anointed, the 'christ', the phallic representative of the ancient fertility god Yahweh/Zeus. His story recounted so vividly in the Gospels was never meant to be read as history by the communities to whom the writings were sent. But embedded in the tale and in the reported words of the legendary teacher were those secret, all-powerful names whose recitation was of such importance for the continuation of the sect's influence, and the freeing or 'salvation' of the souls of the initiates.

In fact, the story itself is full of discrepancies and situations which, to anyone knowing the facts of Jewish religious life and politics, are manifestly absurd. Even the teachings, based as we have noted on Old Testament and current rabbinic precepts, are sometimes treated or expanded in ways that make little sense and seem sometimes downright amoral, not to say immoral. Nevertheless, a cursory reading of the Gospels, setting aside the more obvious extravagances of the 'miracles', gives a generally accurate impression of first-century Palestine, and names are sprinkled through the story, like Herod and Pontius Pilate, which give it added reality. It is only when the historian and philologist comes to look more closely at the details, like the Quirinius census of Luke 2[1ff], placed about a dozen years too early, or the extraordinary antics of the Jewish religious leaders in arranging a 'trial' of Jesus and handing him over to the hated Romans for execution, that credibility becomes strained to breaking point. There are, in fact, difficulties in just about every aspect of the Jesus story; topographical, chronological, and religious, as well as historical and philological.

Conviction of the historicity of the Gospel traditions has been steadily declining among scholars since the beginning of critical research into the Bible. Indeed, it is not uncommon nowadays for a so-called 'liberal' Christian researcher to acknowledge no more fact in the Gospel story than the existence of a teacher called Jesus, and some kind of public ministry culminating in his execution at the hands of the Roman occupying power. The 'miracles' have long ago been attributed more to pious exaggeration on the part of Jesus's followers than hard fact, and even his physical resurrection, on which the Church has largely based its message of hope, has been interpreted by not a few as a resuscitation in the spirit world which left Jesus's mortal remains firmly interred in some lost Palestinian grave.

What we have now to reckon with is the complete disappearance of Jesus of Nazareth from history. However effective this 'cover story' may have been in deceiving the Roman police, so that twenty years or so after it was written the historian Tacitus could repeat the tale of the sect's leader having been executed under Pontius Pilate, the sad fact is that the chief dupes were the Christians themselves, or at least those who inherited that title. The cult they adopted was lacking its prime ingredient, the drug fungus that could bring about their desired union with the Christ.

Instead, as today, they chewed pieces of bread or wafer and sipped new wine, whilst their priests tried to persuade them that they were eating the god's flesh and drinking his blood. The terminology was authentic enough, but the substance bore no more relationship to the real source of the cult's power than, in similar circumstances, the Jewish Passover *mazzoth* represented the dried mushroom tops of the original sacramental meal. The 'events' of the Gospel stories, miracles and all, became essential parts of the Church's dogma, belief in which was as obligatory upon the adherent as was assent to the equally unlikely stories of Adam and Eve, Noah, Moses, etc. upon the post-exilic Jew.

The history of the crucial events of the first and second centuries is unfortunately obscure, not least because the Church destroyed all records and religious works with which its leaders disagreed, or which seemed to cast doubt upon the authority and primacy of the ecclesiastical hierarchy. In particular we should like to know much more about the Gnostic movements of the first century and their previous development. Perhaps there may yet come from the desert original documents from an early Gnostic sect which managed to flee with their precious records intact from the hand of the Church's censors. In the meantime, lacking now even the guide of the New Testament book of Acts, we can but speculate upon the pre-AD 70 Christian communities and the point in time and place where the New Testament narratives became for their custodians the infallible records of the life, death and resurrection of the Son of God.

However, there are indications that the original 'Christian' mushroom cult had not entirely died out even as late as Muhammad's time in the seventh century AD. As has been shown in *The Sacred Mushroom and the Cross*, there are passages and certain words and phrases in the Qur'an (Koran) which would point to the Prophet's having been in contact with the fungus-worshippers and their legends, and may account for some at least of the aberrant forms he received of Christian traditions, as well as the furious energies which his mission released in the Arab world.

What happened to the first 'Christians' is not of prime importance. Much more crucial is the present situation of a civilization which for some two thousand years has been living with, and seeking moral truth and religious comfort from, a lie. Of course, it could be argued that at any time during those centuries intelligent men could have studied the text of the New Testament and realized the gravity of the flaws in the picture it presented. In particular, had scholars not brushed aside the discrepancies between assumed 'Aramaisms' and their 'translations', but probed more deeply into possible botanical references of names like 'Peter' or 'Sons of Thunder', they might at least have wondered if the story of Jesus the martyred rabbi was really to be taken at its face value.

But no religion is an exercise in logical thought or looks for support in pure reason. If a focus for religious aspirations, a projection in myth form of spiritual experience, is all that the New Testament had represented in the Christian world, then the story of Jesus, the suffering Son of God, however unhistorical, is as good as any other. Unfortunately for the western world generally, the New Testament has been made to support far more than purely religious ideology: it has become the fount of moral authority even for people outside the Church. The ethics of the Bible have been made the foundation of western civilization, and that not merely because the moral precepts selected from these Semitic and Greek writings seemed to offer a basis for stable community life, but because they were believed to bear the imprint of God. The Ten Commandments were written by the divine finger and handed to Moses as a guidance to one particular tribe of semi-nomads. They were expanded by a later Israelite, offering with unique authority a new dispensation for men direct from God. For the believer the biblical revelation is inextricably linked with history. The Bible is not a kind of ouija board, conveying without human intervention messages from heaven (though some Jewish and Christian exegetes seem to convey that impression); it was for the believer an infallible record of certain historical events which demonstrate, quite as much as the moral homilies of priests and prophet, God's purpose for the world.

What happens, then, if the supreme act of God's self-revelation, the Incarnation, turns out to be a hoax? Can Christianity exist without Christ? Is the moral teaching of the New Testament really so authoritative if its author was only a word-juggling cryptographer mainly intent on conveying the secrets of a mushroom cult? The Church has constantly to remind its faithful that the Creed was not founded upon the Sermon on the Mount but on the Incarnation. It has insisted on the historicity of the Gospels in the past even in the face of scholarship and common sense; indeed, in times of intellectual difficulties, the Vatican seems to go out of its way to produce dogma even more irrational than that already promulgated, like the Assumption of the Virgin Mary, lacking even biblical support. For the Church has always known that the moral teachings of the New Testament have never really matched the theological importance placed upon their supposed author. There are far more comprehensive, and indeed comprehensible, bodies of homiletics to be found in the classics and in the Eastern religious teachings than in the New Testament. For a start, the words of Jesus, always supposing they had been accurately transmitted and translated over two generations, too often lack context to be of real guidance in any given human situations. Taken at their face value, and without the pious exegesis and expansion that is customarily heaped upon the text from the pulpit, some of them present extremely dubious morality, as for instance, the story of the dishonest steward commended by his master for sagacity (Luke 16), which reads like a charter for crooked accountants.

The Church's theologians have always appreciated that the unique contribution of the Faith has been in its adoration of the god-man Jesus, not his teachings. If the 'Son of God' turns out to have been originally a mushroom, bearer of the 'Word of God', considered to be the semen of the divine penis, does it really matter what the Church later preached as the Gospel, if they had been so mistaken about the historical basis of their faith? Does it matter if the supreme symbol of God's passion for mankind, the Cross, was originally but a representation of the mushroom and, like the fungus, signified the copulation of penis and vulva as the central sacrament of an age-old fertility cult? Can traditional church worship and ceremonial ever be the same if the processional of priests and servers, headed by a cross, down the nave to the altar is now to be recognized as symbolical of the passage of the male organ through the vagina? Can the mystic rite of the eucharist, when the body and blood of the Christ is chewed and imbibed by the celebrant, ever again achieve the same spiritual potency when it is known to be a pale substitute for the partaking of the sacred fungus, whose drug could raise the perceptive levels of the subject to heights beyond normal comprehension? Can a tasteless wafer and watery wine match the ambrosia and nectar of *Amanita muscaria*? In short, can the towering pinnacle of ecclesiastical dogma and authority rest securely on a complete misapprehension of their origins?

For the non-believer the loss of an historical Jesus poses no such theological problems. Nevertheless in a world which has for centuries depended upon the cultural, moral and political leadership of the Church, a sudden upset of the authority of the priesthood must provoke a number of serious situations. Even where religious dogma is not of major concern, a great deal of moral teaching is rooted in biblical ethics as interpreted in the western world. It is interesting to note how agnostic or atheistic debaters on television often show more respect to the Nazarene teacher in this regard than their ecclesiastical opponents. A non-believing politician will quote the Sermon on the Mount to support his argument with blissful assurance that no one will question its authority as supreme arbiter of the social problems of twentieth-century man. To remove the supposed author of these homilies from the field of history is to shake their divine authority and bring their precepts into the range of human debate.

Furthermore, the sudden collapse of ecclesiastical authority in those countries where the Church has long dominated the minds and bodies of an under-privileged peasantry, could spark off a revolution leading to their subjection to an even more authoritarian régime. A power vacuum is an open invitation to a political takeover which, for instance in South America or Italy, could have serious repercussions on the global balance of power.

The fact is that we have reached a crisis in the affairs of western civilization on two fronts. Just at a time when scientific progress threatens us with over-population and a deepening of the rift between rich and poor, the religious sanctions which might have held the situation long enough for the devising of a long-term solution to the economic and social problems are in danger of breaking down completely in mass disillusionment. On the speed of our reaction to this state of affairs depends the future of mankind. It could be that the religious crisis will accentuate the disruptive potential of the economic situation. In this case, only chaos and anarchy can result. On the other hand, a dramatic breakdown in religiously inspired moral authority could lead the way to a reconsideration of the needs of modern man in the new technological situation, freed from the sanctions of a byegone age and social environment. If we can resist the initial impulse to waste time bemoaning the passing of the Ten Commandments and the Sermon on the Mount, we might discover that the common sense that inspired the more practical of their precepts could still serve to produce useful answers to some of our more pressing social and personal problems. We have, in short, reached the end of a road: what lies beyond, chaos or social harmony, rests very largely in our own hands.

CHAPTER THREE

The Church

CHURCH historians talk of a 'tunnel period' in the history of the Church extending from the time of Saint Paul, around AD 40–50, to the supposed date of the first Gospel, about AD 70. During that time nothing is known for certain about the development of the organization, but thereafter the writings of the Church fathers offer some information on the way the hierarchy developed and of the 'heresies' which forced a unification of dogma and practice on the scattered communities. As it now transpires, the period of uncertainty has to be extended far beyond the traditional dates. The Church did not begin in 5 or 6 BC, the supposed date of Jesus's birth, nor in the year AD 33 when he is assumed to have been crucified. The origins of Christianity lay far beyond in the mists of antiquity, as we have shown, and not one identifiable figure emerges from the haze to merit the title of Author of the Faith. As far as the Church is concerned, we have to look for its beginnings in the ascendancy of one sect over several others, in the latter part of the first century. Theologically, it started with the acceptance of the legendary figure Jesus as a real person, and his death and resurrection as marking a crisis and turning point in world history: myth became fact. But, as has been said, the kind of documentary evidence of the struggle that such radical changes must have involved are lost, probably for ever. Extant accounts of arguments with the Gnostic sects are comparatively late and essentially one-sided, hingeing for the most part on less crucial issues of doctrine.

We see the pulling together of the varying shades of belief into a standardized pattern of dogma and practice in the middle of the second century. Diversities in dogmatic formulation and liturgical practice (as in the celebration of Easter), and in the text of Scripture, began to be sorted out to present a common front towards the 'heretical' enemies. The underlying supposition was that since the Church devolved from one man, one revelation, and one God, its organization and teaching must be a unity. Organizationally, the unification of the Church came with the selection of one bishop per city, aided by his presbyters and deacons, and then further centralized with ascendancy to power of the three bishops of the three main centres of the empire, Rome, Alexandria and Antioch. Thus within the historical period, we can trace the transition from a loose confederation of separate communities to a closely-knit and authoritarian organization.

Towards the end of the second century, a further 'regularization' took place in the Church, when the religious phenomenon of 'speaking with tongues', as the New Testament calls it, or babbling under the influence of a drug or hypnosis, became discredited. A Phrygian believer named Montanus, with two female assistants, in an ecstatic trance uttered strange messages which purported to be from the Holy Spirit itself. The Church divided sharply in its appreciation or rejection of this kind of 'instant prophecy', some of the communities holding that the utterances were indeed the word of God, others that they came from the devil. The content of the 'New Prophecy', as it was called, insisted on the literal resurrection of the dead in the flesh, and proclaimed the near approach of the end of the world. The majority of Church opinion treated the phenomenon with suspicion. At Rome the bishop wavered, assailed by protagonists from both sides. One notable convert was the brilliant African orator Tertullian, for whom the puritanism and revivalist messages of the inspired Montanists, as they were called, struck a sympathetic note. He died reviling his former colleagues for putting Church order and authority before what seemed to him to be the living witness of the Spirit.

The majority eventually won that battle. The Catholic Church affirmed its conviction that revelation had come to an end with the apostles and their immediate successors. The last book of the New Testament that could be accorded divine authority had been written. The biblical canon was complete. Of course, in practice within a religious community for whom belief and faith override rational judgement and who maintain that direct communication between the believer and his god is not only possible but highly desirable, such tensions must continually appear. However if every church member is his own priest and prophet, discipline is virtually impossible. Once the confessional grip of the Roman Church was loosened in Europe at the Reformation, and the Bible was translated into local dialects from the 'official' Latin of the Vulgate, the divisive effects that the hierarchy feared from Montanism became evident throughout Christendom. Nowadays anybody believing himself inspired of the Spirit can turn his collar back to front and proclaim himself bishop, priest, deacon and treasurer of a new 'church'.

By the end of the second century, the Church's final weapon against the heresies which assailed its unity was complete. Irenaeus called it the 'Rule of Faith'. It summarized the main events in the cosmic redemptive process, affirming the belief of the one Church in 'God the Father Almighty, maker of heaven and earth and the seas and all that is therein, and in one Christ Jesus the Son of God, who was made flesh for our salvation, and in the Holy Spirit who, through the prophets, preached the dispensations and the comings, and the virgin birth and the passion, and the rising from the dead and the assumption into heaven in his flesh of our Lord Jesus Christ, and his coming from heaven in the glory of the Father ... to raise up all flesh.' Irenaeus asserted the unity of the revelation through the Old Testament to the New; he saw Christ as the second Adam. This one rule, claimed the great defender of orthodoxy, was the substance of the Church's teaching through her bishops, and therefore must have been the teaching of the apostles to whom the present rulers of the Church were the divinely appointed successors.

Tertullian, following Irenaeus, further regarded the 'Rule' as the yardstick by which to judge Scripture, though realizing that it was itself based upon New Testament teaching. Nevertheless, for him the Bible was old and open to many different interpretations; the 'Rule of Faith' was the substance of modern Church belief and therefore must govern the believer's interpretation of the ancient text. The circular argument thus adduced may not be intellectually satisfying, but it laid the theoretical foundations of the Church's authority on scriptural interpretation which has remained to the present day in Catholicism.

So long as the Bible is regarded as verbally inspired and unchangeable, its text fixed in one recension having equal divine authority, and its interpretation controlled by one body of ecclesiastical opinion, all is well. Any difficulties about the meaning of biblical words and passages are simply referred to the central deliberative council, the Latin text studied afresh by the experts, and back comes the answer, final and completely authoritative. It is only when doubts set in about the value of the one selected biblical recension (does it faithfully represent the original Hebrew and Greek? how should one treat important variants within the Hebrew and Greek which are not represented in the Latin? and so on), and worse, when doubts are raised about the historicity of biblical accounts, as occurred a century or so ago with the Darwinian discoveries about the evolution of man and the age of the earth, that the system begins to strain and leak at the seams. Now that Catholic biblical scholarship is fast catching up with scientific literary research in the Bible and in some cases even leading it, the strains are becoming acute. The humble believer, intelligent enough to question the sacred writings, finds that the answers supplied through the ecclesiastical machine are no longer the straightforward, clearcut 'yes-no' decisions he might have expected. He hears of biblical versions contradicting one another, scholarly opinions hesitating between this and that interpretation, even, if he penetrates the united front of the academic boards, of violent squabbles between individuals equally pious and faithful to Mother Church but hopelessly opposed in their conclusions.

The Church is thus in danger of reverting to its pre-Irenaean chaos of a free-for-all in biblical interpretation and a breakdown in centralized interpretative authority. In the Protestant churches, of course, this has long been the case. From the point of view of a unity of belief and witness, the Catholic Church's refusal to countenance the situation when every believer could read the Scriptures in his own tongue has been amply justified. Almost anything can be proved or disproved from the Bible, any action justified by a 'proof-text' dragged from its context. One has only to listen for a few minutes to members of those fringe sects of Christianity who pester busy housewives on their doorsteps to know to what lengths a determined exegete can go in wresting from Scripture 'prophecies' of the end of the world, the Common Market and mini-skirts.

As Essenes could move freely about the country and find hospitality at any of the community centres, so a Christian could be sure of a lodging for up to three nights on production of proof of his faith. Such hospitality was the responsibility of the Essene 'overseer', the Christian 'bishop'. Both accordingly controlled the community's money-bags. In the early Church, the clergy were paid on a dividend system, the total revenues being divided proportionately between the officers. This meant that city churches could pay their clergy much better than rural communities, a not uncommon state of affairs even today. In Rome of the fifth century, the bishop gave himself a quarter of the total revenue; his assistants divided up the remainder between their own stipends, alms to the sick and poor, and the maintenance of church buildings. But it was always understood that alms-giving was the prime object of church revenues and believers were expected to contribute generously of their means to this end. By the middle of the third century the church at Rome was rich enough to support its bishop, 64 presbyters, 7 deacons, 7 subdeacons, 42 acolytes, and 52 exorcists, readers and doorkeepers, and yet to be able to distribute alms to no less than 1,500 widows and needy persons.

Although an illegal organization and thus not permitted to own property as such, the Church perhaps as early as 260 began to receive bequests of money and land, and this practice was legalized by Constantine in 321. From then on the Church became rich in endowments and the income that they provided. In Asia Minor and Syria it became usual to bequeath a fixed proportion of one's property to the Church, even as much as a third. In the West, testators would set aside that part of their wealth as might be left to an additional child. One presbyter of the fifth century foreshadowed modern socialist principles and declared that leaving wealth to one's family at all was the road to damnation. Long before the Church became an organ of State and eventually the State itself, certain of her communities had become very rich indeed, and the administration of that wealth brought its own problems and the need for an organization far outstripping the kind of simple order we see laid down in the administrative rules of the Essenes. Today the Catholic Church is one of the top three property-owning communities in the world, and even the Anglican Church is immensely rich in terms of her City investments, on a par with our largest public companies.

It is easy enough to draw stark contrasts between this kind of wealth and the dabbling in the world's money markets that its manipulation entails, and the professed pauperism of the early Christians, but a large organization like the modern Church requires massive administrative facilities. It is no more real to lay side-by-side the organizational needs of a few scattered communities, each comprising scores or at the most hundreds of members, with the complex 'Pentagon' of the Vatican City, supervising some 423,000,000 adherents, than it is to compare the legendary supper party for thirteen in a loft with High Mass at St Peter's. 'Where two or three are gathered in the Lord's name you have a committee' may be a cynicism, but when religion moves out from being a personal to a communal experience, some kind of organization is required. Sharing a common ritual and mutual exhortation, the basis of institutional Christianity, demands a minimum of physical separation from the outside world, be it only an upper room. Those Christians who today are vociferous in demanding the pulling down of churches and a reversion to primitive worship in people's houses, display either striking realism about the Church's future membership or an unreal optimism about the size of the domestic lounge in modern 'little boxes'.

What the outside spectator must find especially interesting about the current impatience with the monolithic authority of the Vatican and demand for a decentralization of the Church's administration is that it is being raised at the same time as world Christianity is desperately seeking for a common voice to stem the tide of materialism. Just when authority is breaking down and even the papacy is being openly criticized, not to say discredited among intelligent Catholics, Protestant leaders particularly are raising their eyes to a reunited world Church of some 760,000,000 members, Catholic, Orthodox and Protestant. The administrative organization required for such numbers must challenge the most fertile imagination. Furthermore, the hope that such an ecumenical movement would bring a united front to the world's deliberative councils must appear quite unreal to anyone surveying the present religious scene. Never, in some parts of the world, have Protestants been more bitterly opposed to Catholics or more divided among themselves. Theologically they seem farther than ever from finding common ground, since even the biblical basis of the common Creed has never been so subjected to critical scrutiny and uncertainty, let alone variously interpreted by confessional dogma. Quite apart from the dramatic results of our present researches about the nature and origin of Christianity, the biggest obstacle to the much heralded and publicized ecumenical movement in Christendom is that few Christians are sure any longer about what they are supposed to be united in worshipping. This repeated call to a reversion to an original unity of faith, the basis, as we saw, of the standardization of faith and practice in the face of the heresies of the mid-second century, suffers from a lack of confidence within Christian scholarship in the historicity of the Gospel records. After all, how can you ask your hundreds of millions of church members to join together in reaffirming their adherence to a common Creed if the more intelligent and questing of them have long ago decided they do not believe in the Virgin Birth, the resurrection of Jesus on the third day or, for that matter, of any corpse at any time, have extreme doubts about life in the world to come, and are none too sure about the one all-creative Father God. Why, indeed, should the layman be ready to affirm his assent to a biblically based Creed when his scholarly mentors are disputing among themselves about the historicity of large parts of the Gospel traditions?

The fallacy of the ecumenical movement lies in the unity of Christian belief. The great 'Rule of Faith' of Irenaeus and Tertullian was useful as a rallying cry for the faithful against the heresies, and it proved effective. But the heresies were not disproved thereby, merely suppressed. They lived on and, as we may now see, probably bore more relation to the original cult than what came down as 'orthodoxy'. The Rule of Faith was no truer than the Gospel story on which it was based, and that was a hoax, never intended to be taken seriously by the faithful.

Again, orthodoxy won its battle against the Montanist ecstatics. The Church pronounced the age of apostolic prophecy dead. Thereafter interpretation of previously recorded revelation was in the hands of the bishops, spiritual successors to the apostles, loosers and binders of sins, leaders of the Church's discipline and dispensers of her monies, but not prophets. But the genius of the original cult lay in the hallucinatory effects of the drug. Christ was in the worshipper; he had died and been resurrected to new levels of perception with his Lord. To eat the fungus and drink its juice in the sacramental meal was to become one with the Christ. The celebrant was free of the chains of the flesh; his soul floated to the seventh heaven and he saw with the eyes of God. This was a personal, not corporate experience. He might babble strange words whilst in the spirit, and his friends try to interpret them to learn for themselves some of the hidden 'knowledge of God'. He might speak afterwards with human tongue insufficient to convey the wonders of his narcotic experience, and exhort his fellow-members to follow his example. But the experience was his and his alone. It was a personal religion, a mystical relationship with his god which was not controlled by a body of biblical exegetes or bound within the confines of a particular liturgical form of worship. The order and organization of his community of believers, the preservation of the mystic names, the rites which prepared his body and mind for the sacramental meal and the culminating climax of the release of his soul, were means to an end; not the end itself. The goal of every initiate was the losing of himself in God; all else was designed to achieve this ultimate bliss.

To the participant in the mysteries, the world about him was a transient thing. He did not deny its reality; it was the creation of God, and through the earth God had made it possible for the divine essence to be gathered and made the path to enlightenment. The sacred fungus had been conceived in the womb of the earth by God's word. But like the uterus, it was but the organ of generation, the means of new birth, not life itself. Similarly, the community was the womb, the 'bride', to be impregnated by the Spirit and allow the believer to be born again. The material resources of the community were useful only so long as they made it possible for the believer to draw apart from the world, and to keep his soul within his body sufficiently to enable him to use it as a 'launching platform' to the stars.

Although the community which made the mystic's 'trips' into enlightenment possible was of secondary importance to the spiritual experience itself, it was nevertheless important. A discordant environment is of no assistance in the search for the perfect harmony of a mystic's heaven. If the secret of nature's reproductive process lay in the balance of its elements, no less was a balance of possessions and opportunities essential for a community dedicated to the achieving of spiritual harmony. A reflection of this concern with a communism of goods and services is seen in the New Testament, as in the regulations for sharing personal wealth and the establishment of a common fund in the Dead Sea Scrolls. In terms of personal relationships this balance and harmony within the community was sought in the quality we call love.

'See how these Christians love one another', said the pagan, according to Tertullian. Looking about us at the present scene within Christendom, we should repeat the remark only in irony, but doubtless in the second century there were evidences of this communal affection, particularly in alms-giving and care for the sick and aged, that inspired the observation in all sincerity. It is no detraction from the quality of this love that its prime purpose was to ensure the harmony of communal life, and thus to serve the greater ends of religion. Again, love was a means to an end, not the end itself. To call God 'love', as does the Johannine writer in the New Testament, is merely to demonstrate the fundamental thesis of the fertility philosophy, that creation as a continuative process demanded a balance in nature, a cosmic harmony of which the god was the originator and prime controller. That kind of love in human terms finds its most sublime expression in the famous passage in I Corinthians 13, beginning, 'If I speak in the tongues of men and of angels, but have not love, I am a noisy gong or a clanging cymbal . . . love is patient and kind, is not jealous or boastful . . .' and so on.

Within a community founded on a love philosophy, enmity between the brethren was at all costs to be avoided. In the New Testament the essence of the biblical proverb, 'a soft answer turneth away wrath' (Prov. 15^1) is expanded to a doctrine of non-retaliation whose object is always the preservation of harmony. Some elements of the Church have taken this precept to absurd lengths of self-abasement and so-called pacifism, the end result of which is to achieve a violent imbalance between individuals and nations and inevitable disaster. Valuable as this conception of brotherly love and patience was within the closely-knit society if the ends of religion were to be achieved, it does not mean that the cult had no enemies. Apart from the political foes on whom the New Testament calls down fire and consigns to utter damnation, and who wrought such havoc among the communities by persecution, there were in the universe, they believed, far greater powers of evil seeking all the time to destroy their souls. The combating of these satanic influences apparently formed a large part of Gnostic hocus pocus, including the recitation of the divine names and the 'our-Father-which-art-in-heaven' Abracadabra incantation previously mentioned.

We may probably seek the origin of part at least of the very real fear of the angels of darkness in the extreme dangers into which drug-taking led the initiates of the mystery cults. The aim of the exercise was, as we have said, the release of the soul from the body so that it could fly away to heaven and experience hallucinations beyond the realm of normal perception. But as we are only too well aware these days, this drug-taking is a dangerous and extremely foolish practice. Worshippers of the sacred fungus chewed a mushroom which, although fairly harmless in small quantities, can be fatal in large doses. We are told by modern observers that the Siberian devotees of the mushroom cult dried the tops of the *Amanita muscaria* in the sun or over a hearth, and were then able to take between three and ten at one time without deadly effect. But three fresh fungi was said to be sufficient to kill a man. In *The Sacred Mushroom and the Cross* we showed how the administration of the drug was controlled according to the supposed susceptibilities of the individual, determined by his astrological 'forecasts', that is, his characteristics, physical and mental, as indicated by the time and place of birth in the Zodiac. The mistakes must have been numerous. Estimating the right amount of antidote to be mixed with the drug must have posed serious problems. Furthermore, one effect of the drug is to throw the subject into a violent frenzy during which he might well injure himself and anyone within reach.

The natural explanation for such 'accidents' would certainly have been that the departure of the subject's spirit had permitted the entry into his vacant body of demonic powers intent on harm, and examples abound of this kind of reasoning in the New Testament stories of epileptics. Again, whilst the spirit wings its way aloft, it is itself dangerously vulnerable. The Gnostics speak of its having to find its way through the seven heavens to its goal, at each stage beset by demons which can be countered only by powerful incantations. We may reasonably connect this with the seven stages of initiation of the Mithraic cult, and the seven 'churches of Asia' of Revelation (1[4]), where 'Asia' is a pun on a Semitic word for 'healing' in its wider, religious sense of 'salvation'.

The devils which sought to lure away the naked soul were using the arts of 'fascination', the 'evil eye' as it is known the world over. As we have shown elsewhere, the origin of the word 'fascinate' lies in the sexual power exerted by women over the male organ, causing it to erect apparently without the acquiescence or control of its owner. The ancient distrust of women and the ascription by the Church to the sex of demonic powers and the hounding of witches are reflections of the fearfulness with which the ancients viewed this power of 'fascination'. The word was extended to any form of control without visible means, and the all too patent fact that many a freed soul did not return to its body was taken as evidence that somewhere in its long and hazardous journey it had been bewitched and lured away to destruction or to eternal wandering in the heavenly spheres.

The Christians, and later the Church, have always been surrounded with enemies, temporal and spiritual. The blood-curdling phraseology of parts of the New Testament only match the remorseless use of the sword and fire by the Church of the Middle Ages against the enemy without, the Muslims, and the enemy within, the 'heretics' who faced the Inquisition. Side by side with this violent accompaniment to the acquisition of power and material wealth, there existed the more pacific aspect of monasticism. This movement which renounced the world and dedicated itself to the service of God was, of course, much closer in practice and intent to the original nature of the mystery cults. The enemy here was primarily spiritual, those devils of the flesh who tried to bar the soul from full communion with God. It was in such communities that the doctrine of brotherly love and harmony was practised and evoked the commendation of pagan outsiders.

In the Essenes of Qumran by the Dead Sea and the Therapeutae of Egypt we see manifestations of the same monastic movement in closely related religious organizations. As the quietist Essenes of Palestine had their counterparts in the so-called 'Zealots' who could not rest until their madness had brought Judaism and its Temple down about their ears, so the monastics of the Church suffered the activities of their empire-building popes and heard the name of their Prince of Peace bawled as a battle cry on the blood-soaked fields of Europe and Palestine.

The tension within the Church arising from these two extremes of quietism and militancy has never been entirely resolved. They represent two sides of human nature and, in particular, two aspects of the original cult. The frenzied activity which is induced by the drug is preceded and followed by periods of calm, so intense that it became proverbial. Ancient writers speak of 'the Bacchic silence' which, as we showed in *The Sacred Mushroom and the Cross*, probably derives from this abnormal lethargy that comes over the participant in the drug-rites of the sacred fungus after periods of lunatic exertion. In fertility philosophy terms, it represented in a peculiarly intense form the exhaustion that follows the climax of the sex act, the calm and joy that follows parturition, the softness of the atmosphere after the storm. In any profound religious experience there are moments of great excitement and periods of peace, often of a depressant nature. The Catholic Church in its two great pillars of the papacy and monasticism represented from the earliest times this inner conflict of the spirit, as if the vigorous, self-righteous determination of the militant arm had to be compensated for by the soul-searching doubts and confessionals of the quietist. Facile judgements about the comparative good and evil inflicted upon the human race by each branch of the Church are to be avoided; neither was free from faults. It would be difficult to maintain that the good that either has performed has adequately compensated for the restriction Catholic authoritarianism has imposed upon the mind of Western man and for the circumscribing of the range of his intellectual enquiry. Perhaps in this respect the inward-looking monastic, despite his valuable literary activities, did less to stimulate fresh advances in knowledge than the papal despot who sent his armies with bloody swords to protect his empire. They at least came back knowing a little more of the world at large, even if their religious fervour had decimated its population.

CHAPTER FOUR

Unity of Belief and Action

THE Pope and the Roman Catholic hierarchy derive their authority from the apostles. At first this commission mainly concerned the proper interpretation of the Old and New Testaments and the regulation of conflicting notions about what the Christian was supposed to believe. Ignatius of Antioch (martyred before AD 117) insisted that the local bishop was God's representative on earth and therefore could reasonably be accepted as 'the Lord himself'. However, some more direct connection between Jesus as Author of the Faith and the bishops who mediated his teachings was clearly needed.

About the end of the first century, the church members of Corinth staged a revolution against the clergy, deposed the incumbents and replaced them by new men. This brought forth a serious protest from the authorities of Rome in the form of a letter claiming divine inspiration, from one Clement, probably the bishop or presbyter of the church of that city. He besought the Corinthian community to avoid disrupting the unity of the faith by deposing those who stood in due succession to the apostles of Jesus. The importance of this edict, which apparently convinced the malcontents of the error of their ways, was that it carried the implication that the bishops knew all there was to know about the divine revelation of the Lord to his followers. Whatever Peter and Paul had learnt of consequence from Jesus in the flesh or spirit they would have passed on to those they ordained as leaders of the Christian communities, who in turn would have transmitted the information to their successors. Outside this 'apostolic succession' there could be therefore no true revelation. The need for this limitation of received tradition lay in countering Gnostic claims to possessing teaching supposed to have been imparted by Jesus to his apostles during the forty days of his life in the flesh after the resurrection and which did not appear in the Gospels. It had been transmitted only through the Gnostic teachers, thus putting them in the advantageous position of knowing more than the leaders of the 'orthodox' sect. This dangerous heresy, which threatened to open the doors to complete confusion among the believers about the content of Jesus's teaching, could only be stopped by ascribing to the bishops complete authority over what was and what was not the word of the Lord. Their teaching had to be accepted as identical with that of the first apostles, whether it was written down in the Gospels, or conveyed orally as a collection of the Master's sayings. The bishops were thus, in this respect, the very mouthpiece of God, their teaching infallible.

The theory found its most clear-cut and uncompromising form with Irenaeus, towards the end of the second century. In his arguments with the Gnostics he claimed that he could vindicate orthodox tradition by appealing to an unbroken succession of teachers in any one of the apostolically derived churches. He quotes as a particularly good example the case of the church at Rome, and traces back its foundation to Peter and Paul, traditionally believed to have been martyred there. So clear is this line of succession, so evident the rightness of teaching there, the believer need look nowhere else for proof of this infallible transmission of the Lord's teachings, although it could as well be seen in Ephesus or Corinth or the others. Thus the Christian, wherever he may be, may rest assured that the true teaching of the Church may be discovered without doubt from the lips of the bishops; no deviation in doctrine was at all conceivable. How very different, Irenaeus urged, from the conflicting notions of the Gnostics. None of the sects agreed with one another, whereas the true Church was one in theology and in its Bible and interpretation, as it was in its God and Saviour.

Unfortunately for the theory, diversity of views about almost every aspect of Church life, discipline and order, and the interpretation of the Bible continued to exist despite the supposed unbroken apostolic succession. Indeed, the sceptic could hardly fail to notice that even the four Gospels differed in detail from one another, and in the case of the fourth, John, markedly so from the other three, the so-called Synoptics. And the story of Acts hardly reads like the history of one undivided brotherhood of believers, affirming the same undeviating teaching of their Lord. If the witness of the church at Rome were really derived from a single, homogeneous revelation through Peter and Paul, one would have to suppose a remarkable reconciliation between these pillars of the Church and their divergent opinions not readily discernible in the New Testament.

Nevertheless, the timely arguments of Irenaeus and his followers saved the Church from falling apart in discord. We may wonder, looking back, at the gullibility of those who apparently accepted the arguments and 'proof' adduced, and how, knowing the bishops concerned and the discrepancies which must have often been detected in their teaching, the opinion that these were the mouthpieces of God and conveyors of an unbroken and infallible apostolic teaching could have survived. Nevertheless, the Papacy still maintains its authority on what is now quite certainly a fictitious list of bishops reaching back to the apostle Peter. The constant efforts made by the Church's historians to support the traditions that Peter went to Rome, and even the recent 'discovery' of the apostle's bones under St Peter's, must seem rather foolish in the light of our recent enquiries. The 'Peter' of the Gospel myth was a mushroom, his existence and name a projection of the old Semitic name of the fungus, *pitra*. The authority that the story gives him as a 'key of the kingdom' was simply a fanciful development by word-play of an ancient name of the mushroom as the 'bolt-herb' (a reference to its having the shape of the knobbed penis), combined with the belief that the fungus could open the gates to heaven for the initiate. The cultic title Cephas by which he is otherwise known was certainly that of an administrative office, and is found elsewhere attached to a Jewish priest, but its use in the New Testament story owes far more to a pun between this word and another name for the mushroom, *cepa*, and between a similar Aramaic word for 'stone', *cepha*, and another pun on the Greek *petros*, *petra*, of similar meaning.

One is forced to the conclusion that in those early centuries, when both politically and intellectually the Church was under severe pressure, the first need of the believers was for assurance that they were right and their opponents wrong. They gratefully seized upon this obvious fiction of the unbroken apostolic lineage of their leaders because amid all the uncertainties of their position they had to have a fount of unquestionable authority.

In Egypt, the more educated sections of the Church were troubled by the contrast between the sophistication of Greek pagan philosophy and the somewhat artless, even crude, writing of the Bible. It was Clement, at the end of the second century, who overcame their embarrassment by expressing biblical themes in Greek philosophical terms. He explained that Plato had plagiarized Moses and the prophets without due acknowledgement, and that Greek philosophy, like the Mosaic Law, was a necessary step towards the fuller understanding offered the Christian. He summarized the Sermon on the Mount in terms of neo-Pythagorean gnomic wisdom, without relating it verbally to the New Testament text. In short, he made the Bible 'respectable' to the over-sensitive Alexandrian intellectual. The fact that his treatment of the Semitic writings in this way was grotesquely unreal, displaying an utter contempt for the genius of the Old Testament, was immaterial; he offered the Egyptian sophisticate what he needed most: an assurance that his faith was as intellectually defensible as the Gnostic speculations.

This almost desperate search in the early Church for an intellectual justification for believing something at heart quite irrational is particularly interesting at the present time. We are now seeing among intelligent laymen an equally intensive movement in the opposite direction: that is, a search for an intellectually respectable reason for ceasing to believe. Many Christians, brought up in the Faith and persuaded that it is the only means by which they can remain true to their ethical ideals, have nevertheless discovered they are no longer able to convince themselves that they believe the basic tenets of the Christian confession. They find the Church's blessings of comforting self-assurance too high a price for the sacrifice of their intellectual integrity. For some time they have ceased to recite the Creed in church, pondering on the words with increasing incredulity as it is murmured around them. They have listened to the priest's intoning of the Epistles, Sunday by Sunday, with growing conviction that he understands the phrases no more than his audience. Furthermore, the doubter is well aware, if he has troubled to follow the trends in biblical criticism and theological speculation, that the ideal of one Church with one scriptural tradition and one episcopal channel of apostolic truth is further from realization today than it ever was. The monolithic dogma sought by the early Church was never more than a pious hope. It succeeded in imposing a kind of confessional unity on the scattered communities largely because their members wanted it so; it is easier to believe one voice with one point of view than to be obliged to choose between many conflicting notions. But in these days the cracks in even the Roman Church's façade are so wide that even the most myopic and uncritical layman can hardly fail to notice them. It is even fashionable openly to criticize the Pope, let alone his pronouncements, and to accuse him of failing to understand the needs of his flock. Such basic Church disciplines as the celibacy of the clergy are brought openly into public debate, and the increasing numbers of ordained priests leaving the Church to marry, while still stoutly maintaining their adherence to the Faith and their willingness to serve the Church, hardly presents an example of theological solidarity to the bewildered laity.

So, many a disillusioned Christian, sadly aware that the Faith and Church no longer command his allegiance, seeks an excuse for leaving. He is often among the most vociferous critics of the priesthood, claiming that they are more concerned with theological niceties than the crying needs of humanity. He takes them to task for their insistence upon the primacy of worship, for the care of the church fabric, for liturgical aesthetics, and so on, when they might be declaiming the social injustices of the time, building homes for the homeless, stopping wars and sponsoring Oxfam-type operations to relieve famine. He is taken aback when the Pope decrees once again the sinfulness of contraception at a time when the world faces perhaps its greatest challenge of over-population. And on a more local level he grumbles to his friends (but never to the priest) that he has not had a pastoral visit from the clergy for months.

In point of fact, the unhappy man seeks only a scapegoat to excuse his own disillusionment. If he thought about it he would realize that the priesthood was not ordained to run Oxfam, or a hippie clinic, or a building society, or any of the other much-needed humanitarian enterprises. The priest was ordained as a minister of religion, to guide and strengthen the relationship between his flock and himself and God. The Church is primarily a community of believers, and only secondarily a dispenser of charity. The priest may believe that fostering a mystical relationship with the deity leads to good works. Unhappily, the history of religion generally and Christianity in particular makes this a doubtful proposition; the anguished cries of souls broken on the rack of conformity or on the field of battle, or wrung from tired, dispirited women torn apart with the cares and responsibilities of unwanted pregnancies, make a mockery of such claims. Nevertheless, religion is religion; the priest is a servant of his god. The cold, stark answer to the doubter is to doubt, and get out.

One wonders how much the well-publicized ecumenical movement within the churches stems from similar intellectual disillusionment with the tenets of the Faith, rather than a genuine desire to chase this will-o'-the-wisp of confessional unity. We hear its protagonists on every side castigating unmercifully those who are not willing to throw aside the traditions of their chosen denominations. 'Hidebound', 'obscurantists', 'prepared to sacrifice this glorious opportunity of a unity of believers for petty denominational prejudices', are the accusations levelled at Methodists who do not want to be Anglicans, and Anglicans who have no wish to drift closer and closer to Rome. The wondering, not to say incredulous, outsider watches this pantomime of universal brotherhood as fully aware as its promoters in their moments of reality that religious differences are among the most divisive forces in human society. Once the Reformation destroyed the monolithic aspect of the Roman Church and put the Bible into the hands of every layman, the Irenaean concept of one authority, one scriptural tradition and interpretation, had gone for ever. The proliferation within Protestantism of hundreds and thousands of different sects was inevitable. This was always the nightmare of the Church fathers: the chaotic diversities of Gnostic belief, each claiming infallibility and dependance upon apostolic tradition, was on every side a hideous warning of what might happen to the Church unless some kind of unity was imposed upon the communities. In the second century urgent steps were taken, and for the time being the battle was won, because the faithful wanted it so. At the Reformation a war-torn Europe was tired of papal despotism; unity under tyranny was no blessing and was discarded. But at that moment in the Church's history the seeds of doubt and discord were sown, and the flower has confirmed the worst fears of the early leaders.

There can be no going back. If the Methodists ever do unite with the Anglicans, and their Synod Chairmen sport the purple, a new 'Primitive Methodism' will arise within a year to sing their Sankey and Moody hymns and listen spell-bound to their lay-preachers declaiming 'in the Spirit' against the hideous machinations of the 'scarlet women of Rome'. The Baptists will continue to regard with contempt the baptism of infants by the Anglican priests, and the Anglicans will be thankful they do not have to step into a bath up to their neck to demonstrate their allegiance to the Lord. In short, religion is so personal an emotion that conformity in its outward and inward manifestation can never be a realistic aim. Our ecumenical reformers may succeed in throwing a single veil of unity over large sections of Christendom, but beneath it the old divisions will continue. They may even be able to persuade the poorer churches to sell their buildings for Bingo halls and economize by sharing the running expenses of a single place of worship. In that event one can forsee the erstwhile 'evangelical' believers making the removal of candles, crucifixes, and other hideous examples of 'papist' regalia a necessary preliminary to their own fiercely anti-liturgical 'meetings'. In the end the cloying smell of stale incense will drive them to build their own wooden shed on someone's garden allotment, and the whole story of Gnostic heresies will begin again.

But is the ecumenical movement really a revolt against the

divisions of the Church, and not in reality a rebellion against religious institutionalism itself? In seeking to break down the denominational divisions, are these earnest men and women not in fact resisting the very discipline of uniformity they ostensibly seek to reimpose? They are impatient with a Church which appears to stand by powerless as mankind drives remorselessly on to self-destruction. They see starving women and children crying for bread whilst the Church waxes fat on its City dividends and at the same time launches appeals for millions of pounds to save its cathedrals from the death-watch beetle. They see emergent black nations engaged in pitiless civil wars, and the great nuclear powers glowering at one another over the tables of the United Nations, whilst the Pope flutters around the world plaintively calling for peace.

The ecumenists long for Christendom to speak with a single voice against the inhumanities of man. But whose voice? Their fallacy is that of Irenaus: there is no single Faith derived from one Lord. Even had there been an historical Jesus, and his words accurately transmitted and infallibly recorded, their interpretation and relevance to any given situation must be the activity of fallible men. The South African Boer is as certain that his black servant was divinely ordained to remain subservient to his white master as Father Huddlestone and his friends are convinced that Christianity preaches otherwise. Prime Minister Churchill had no more doubt about the one God's support for his country in 1940 than had the German field padres on the other side of the Channel.

If, in his most wildly optimistic moments, the ecumenist is convinced that the one Spirit will eventually break through man's prejudice and selfishness and guide all Christians to a common solution of the world's problems, he must be reminded again that this mystical direct communication between the believer and God gave rise in the Church's early days to the

Montanist heresy which split the communities of Asia Minor from the western Church for a century. The 'New Prophecy' then was condemned because of its divisive, not its unifying, effects. The age of prophetic revelation was declared dead. Thenceforth the bishops would alone transmit the apostolic traditions, and their interpretation of the revelation was authoritative for the whole Church. In short, logically, the only form of ecumenism that can be effective and remain true to patristic teaching is a reunification of the 'free' churches with Rome under the primacy of the Pope, an end devoutly to be wished by the Vatican but hardly likely to commend itself to the Protestant churches now being urged to join forces.

Are the divisions of the Church the 'scandal' or 'stumbling-block' that the ecumenists assert them to be? Do people fall away from membership because there exist so many different sects of Christendom, unable to see eye to eye even on matters of doctrinal importance? Surely the intelligent enquirer would be far more suspicious of a single organization claiming to be the channel of an intensely personal faith like Christianity and the mouthpiece of hundreds of millions of people of many races and colours. An extraordinary feature of Christianity has been the ability of people of so many different outlooks to interpret the man Jesus in terms of their own heroic mythology. It is nonsense to pretend that this common focus of worship on to a single figure has produced a monolithic faith. There are as many varieties of 'Christianity' as there are national churches. The words of their liturgies may sound the same or derive from a common tongue, but their interpretations are different, their manner of worship varies with the racial characteristics and local needs of the converts. Nineteenth-century missionaries were as gratified with the speedy integration of the white man's god into the natives' pantheon as they were soon horrified by the rôles Jesus was expected to play in their tribal fertility rituals.

It is commonly said that Christianity would gain respect and even converts if the Church's leaders could speak with one voice on humanitarian matters. The statesmen of the world would hush their wrangling and stay their fingers from the nuclear buttons if there rose before them the awful majesty of the Church, condemning war and hatred and preaching love. But why should a Muslim or a Hindu or a Buddhist, or an adherent of any of the other great religions of the world, pay any more attention to this spokesman of a World Church than they did to the Pope on his recent visit to the United Nations? Is it conceivable that hundreds of millions of people of dozens of different nationalities, economic needs, racial characteristics, and so on, are going to discover simultaneously a common solution to their problems and authorize this mighty voice to convey it to a world council?

The ecumenist surely seeks not for a unity of religion but a unity of humanitarian purpose. He calls on Christians to forget their denominational differences and raise their eyes to behold the Nazarene teacher. Unfortunately, the New Testament offers very little for the believer to behold. The actions depicted of Jesus convey a very mixed impression: on the one hand we have the gentle shepherd calling boys and girls to his knee; on the other we see him using a lash upon perfectly respectable money-changers in the Temple courts where they had every right to be, and without whose services the Jewish religious taxes could not have been collected. We hear him speaking of a just God punishing the wicked, but when confronted with the real day-to-day problem of law enforcement by corporal punishment, he sidesteps the issue by inviting the adulteress's judges to cast the first stone only if they are themselves free from sin, making a mockery of all judicial procedures. At a time when the most burning issue was whether a Jew's obligations to God should allow him to pay taxes to the hated occupying power, the

Teacher's only advice was to 'render to Caesar the things that are Caesar's, and to God the things that are God's', which would have left the questioner precisely where he was and, in real life, very probably the Nazarene with a knife in his back or at best, spittle in his eye.

In all these cases, and indeed in practically every word and action recorded of Jesus, some interpretative comment is required for the action to have relevance for different times and circumstances, or even comprehensibility. Thus, the New Testament picture of Jesus cannot, as is so often piously affirmed, be left to speak for itself. To raise the eyes to the Nazarene teacher is insufficient guidance to offer the Christian beset with the world's present problems, and it is in the varied interpretations of the life and teaching of Jesus that Christendom is most divided.

If then, as we may suspect, the intention of the energetic ecumenist is to urge common action by the churches for humanitarian purposes, he would do better, paradoxically enough, leaving religion out of his calculations. It would be tragic if all the goodwill and effort that is presently being directed towards finding a common religious basis for solving our pressing social and international problems should be dissipated in continued wrangling between theologians over what must now be regarded as a dead letter. The 'Jesus' to whom the believers are directed to lift their eyes was originally a phallic mushroom; the cult which worshipped him was a sex-drug religion which at its best served only to deceive weak-minded individuals into thinking they were gods, and at its worst led them to band together in dangerous and futile attempts to wrest world power from their governors. However different the Church may have become by abandoning its original motivation and historicizing its own mythology, an ecumenical movement which hopes for unity by harking back to a fantasy is bound to fail.

Like the disillusioned church member who cannot now believe

the Church's dogma but wants to safeguard the moral standards of himself and his children, the ecumenist needs to find a new rationale for his humanitarianism, which is, after all, only applied ethics.

CHAPTER FIVE

Religion and Morals

PERHAPS the greatest single effect of our new understanding of the origins of Christianity will be to make us look again at the relationship between religion and morality. For most people 'Christianity' is synonymous with 'ethics', and in particular with a view of life which emphasizes the superiority of people to things and the necessity of tolerance and understanding in our dealings with each other. 'Christianity', we say, 'is loving our neighbour'; it is the religionist who adds 'because God is love, and demonstrated that love by sending His only-begotten Son to offer us salvation'. Thus the vast majority of people separate the human relationship from its religious sanction. However much the theologian may regard the one as dependent upon the other, asserting that there is no Christianity without Christ, the non-believer can quite easily point to demonstrations of 'Christian' charity by pagans happening all round him every day, and at the same time cite acts of Christian non-charity and bigotry which he would say the world could well do without. The theologian will reply by saying that the pagan's 'Christianity' has been learnt from the precept and example of the better exemplars of the Faith, and whilst acknowledging and deploring the lapses of history, draws a distinction between the ideal to which the Christian aspires and the unrepresentative failures to reach it.

The argument is interminable and now largely pointless. There is certainly in the western world particularly, a tradition of neighbourliness which may have been fostered by the quietist divisions of the Church, preaching and practising unselfishness, consideration for other people, particularly the poor and helpless, and finding that attitude exhorted by certain parts of Scripture. Pagan philosophies similarly call for self-renunciation and devotion to the needs of others. It is not difficult to trace the religious basis for this kind of love. As we saw, the philosophical foundation of the fertility religion was the balance of nature, and its maintenance by the combined efforts of the god and man. God provided lavishly of his gifts, but if man wasted them or failed to make provision for the lean years, greedily taking and never giving, retribution was inevitable. If one man became rich at the expense of his fellows, he would drive the oppressed man to despair and revenge. The balance that the agriculturist needed to preserve in the rotation and conservation of his crops was reflected in his dealings with other human beings. Community life is only possible when needs are balanced by giving, and gifts by restraint.

The giving of alms in Judaism, Christianity and Islam has always been a religious exercise: in Hebrew 'righteousness' and 'alms' are synonymous. The Christian bishop's first call upon the collection box was provision for the poor, and the kind of lavish splendour with which he began to surround himself from the fourth century on was at first considered a reproach to the Church. If we really want to find a religious justification for charitableness, even in its widest sense, it is very simply in this fundamental thesis of the fertility philosophy, that the creative process cannot continue unless the natural world is maintained in a state of balance. Whether you believe that the source of life is a mighty penis in the sky ejaculating semen every time it rains, or some philosophic First Principle, an eternal Logos, the practical need for equilibrium in the universe is as patently evident now as ever it was. Does one have to ascribe personality and will to this principle to help us achieve it? Perhaps for some, personal restraint over those primal needs of the body, food and sex, demands the sanction of fear of divine retribution, or the conscious effort to please the deity at the cost of personal sacrifice or discomfort. Some people are literally unable to keep away from carbohydrates without 'slimming' pills. Some women renounce the use of contraceptives voluntarily because only the fear of unwanted pregnancy or social disgrace will keep them 'chaste'. There are, then, people for whom a personal religion is necessary for the maintenance of a moral life; in this case it seems religious discipline and morals are in practice inseparable.

On the other hand, to go on confusing the issue by maintaining, with the Church and other interested parties, that the one is indispensable to the other is not only obviously untrue but poses unnecessary and dangerous barriers to the achievement of a universal ethic. Somehow or other the western 'Christian' world must come to terms with the rest of humanity. If its leaders are going on privately believing that the best we can achieve is a working relationship and the avoidance of open conflict until such time as the Buddhist renounces Buddha for Christ, and the Muslim is willing to demote Muhammad from No. 1 in the prophetic charts to No. 2 (or, better, somewhere below Moses), we shall make little progress. It is fashionable to assert that the Christian has long outlived his desire to convert the world; that he readily accepts these days that one man's god is as good as another, all are seeking the same goal and each has something to contribute to the search for ultimate truth, and so on. It all sounds well enough and refreshingly tolerant after the blood baths in the cause of Christian evangelism of former ages. But this is not the view of orthodox Christian theology. Jesus Christ was the Son of God, presenting in Himself a completely unique and sufficient revelation of the Father to the world. Jesus was God. Since there is only one deity, there can only be one likeness to reveal, and in Jesus the world of the first century and the believer of all succeeding centuries could see the Father. It follows that however near other revelations could have come to portraying the nature of God, only in Jesus could that picture be seen to perfection. Thus the Church claims to be the medium of perfect truth; she, and she alone, has access to the Father through the Son, and in the Church alone can man find salvation.

To the non-believer, and particularly to the adherent of another religion, all this sounds intolerably bigoted, but at least he has to admit it is logical. If you start off with the assumptions of the Christian you must end with the Church's conclusions that she alone has access to knowledge of God: all other revelations are but pale imitations of the real thing. The ecumenical protagonist tends to jolly everyone along with some rather loose talk about the essential unity of Christianity and how but a thin veil separates the various denominations from each other and from the other world religions. Then suddenly the Vatican will make a statement about the essential truth purveyed by Catholicism, inferring the second-rate nature of all other confessions within Christendom and all religions without, that comes as a sharp jolt of reality and stops the wave of brotherly feeling dead in its tracks. Rome cannot compromise, whether it be in matters of apostolic succession or birth control. What Rome's critics, within and without the Church, fail too often to appreciate is that the authority of the Church from the second century has been based on episcopal discipline. The bishops knew better than anyone what was right for the Church in matters of dogma and conduct, and in due course final authority came to rest on the bishop of the Rome community. To question that authority is to question the wisdom of God. To allow the Pope's decisions to be openly debated, let alone modified to suit the wishes of the laity or the needs of the world at large, however pressing, is to wreck the whole disciplinary and moral structure of the Church.

Similarly, it is inconceivable that the Roman Church could allow its members' moral conduct to be subject to the dictates of any other body. It is useless to pretend that the world will ever see the Holy Father sitting down at a table with the President of the World Council of Churches, the Secretary-General of the United Nations, the Chairman of the USSR, the President of the United States and the Archbishop of Canterbury, to debate whether abortion ought to be made freely available, or contraceptives sold in Sicilian supermarkets, or doctors authorized to kill the insane, the incurably sick or unwanted parents in their dotage. If asked, the Pope would doubtless be happy to offer from a distance his advice on these and many other matters to such an authoritative body; but he would not expect to debate the affair, at least not outside his own hierarchy.

Thus, although one may acknowledge the help some people receive from their religion in moral questions requiring self-discipline, we should not expect to find in any one faith a universal ethic. No religious dogma ever revealed or invented can answer all our problems, and every day now there are new ones being posed by advances in technology and medicine which must defy the ingenuity of the most resourceful biblical exegete. The old exhortations to love one another and to hold life sacred sufficed to cover most human situations, at least so long as the practical application of the general precept seemed conducive to peace and the well-being of the majority. But nowadays we have grown more distrustful of general principles; history has shown that more unhappiness and hatred have come from the short-sighted application of principles to delicately poised human situations than from any other source. It is not a cynicism to say that moral principles are fine where they are drawn wide enough to leave room for diplomatic manoeuvre. It is too easy to forget in moments of high moral dudgeon that the other chap has principles too, and the end of the encounter must be another Viet Nam or dockers' strike, unless the even greater principle of equilibrium is made paramount.

We saw earlier that the practical worth of the old axiom of 'loving one's neighbour' is largely dependent on how one means 'love' in any given situation. If, as was suggested, it relates to a maintenance of a balance of interests between people, giving and receiving with a greater concern for the other person than oneself (you can give too much, and take too unwillingly), then 'loving' is a rare art and very far removed from the sloppy sentimentalism it is so often depicted.

Similarly, to promote 'the sanctity of life' to a fundamental principle, whether of medicine or social administration, can have disastrous results. Again, it sounds well enough, and with the gas chambers of the German concentration camps and the blanket bombing of European cities still too fresh in our memories, it is an attractive over-simplification of the human problem. The Christian sees it as a natural corollary to the doctrine of the fatherhood of God: all men are His children, of equal worth in His eyes, and therefore all human life is sacred to God. Like the old fertility religion, Catholicism goes back a stage further: God is life, represented in the spermatozoa that fertilizes the egg, therefore semen is sacred and the life that it creates in the uterus is a gift of God and thus inviolable. Quite logically, then, contraception is wrong; life at whatever stage must be preserved. If it is a choice between the life of the 'receptacle' of this grace, the mother, or the foetus, the new life must be preserved. In giving the sacred sperm a nest, the woman has fulfilled her greatest mission and is dispensable.

Even women have to admit this reasoning is logical, given the first assumptions. But their unwillingness in modern times to act as walking wombs, whose only or even main function is to bear young for the benefit of their mates, is at last throwing into relief the main objection to this beautifully logical theory: a woman is not a sow. In the last few decades she has begun to assert herself and to voice her resistance to being looked upon by the dominant male as a cooker of dinners and bearer of children. These days many intelligent women combine with parenthood a vivid interest in social affairs and hold honoured positions in the professions. In such cases the possibility that her life might be forfeit in the hands of a Catholic doctor in order to save an unborn foetus must surely shake the parents' faith in the Church's basic assumptions, if not in her logic. The general principle of the sanctity of human life is all right as far as it goes. But in practice it has to be qualified: there is life, and life. The hard fact of experience shows that lives are *not* of equal worth. We may shrink from decisions involving the sacrifice of one life for another, or from making comparisons between their relative value to society. But sometimes these decisions have to be made, and in the future many more such painful dilemmas will face ordinary people, as we shall see. In such cases we cannot refer merely to a general principle, and even the most faithful Catholic, in such an extreme situation as that cited above, would doubt the wisdom of a Church that demanded that a beloved wife and mother, a contributor to the intellectual as well as domestic life of the community, should be sacrificed for a foetus.

Much more common is the Catholic's dilemma over contraception. Behind the Church's ban is, as we have said, the same general principle of the sanctity of life, or 'natural law'. In the recent papal encyclical the Vatican is being perfectly logical and true to itself. It cannot compromise on this issue. The fact that it has in fact already done so, in advocating the so-called 'safe period' for sexual intercourse without intent to procreate, is a flaw in the Church's consistency which has not helped her in the present crisis. For to ejaculate semen into a womb that is known to be temporarily barren is no less 'sinful' in its proper, religious sense than barring the ingress of sperm by physical means.

Nevertheless there was no logical reason why hard-pressed Catholic women should have hoped for any different result from the Vatican's deliberations about the Pill than about any other form of birth-control. The decision was not asked for on humanitarian grounds; it is, religiously speaking, not the point that parents should wish to plan conception according to their circumstances, nor that governments of over-populated countries with large Catholic communities would wish to stem the ever-growing human tide until they can cope with the feeding problem. The religious principle of the sanctity of life is paramount. Human anguish and misery, starvation and bloody revolution, and the other fearful results which might well stem from the papal decree are not religiously relevant. God has decreed the Pill sinful.

The rest of the world may beat its breast and bewail the crass stupidity of it all. We may wonder what manner of people are these Catholics who allow a celibate priest to decree when and how they may copulate. But we, like they, must acknowledge that its religious logic is unanswerable. It is difficult to find sympathy with those vociferous members of the Church who protested publicly against the decision at the time of its promulgation, and yet claimed to be still good Catholics. The whole basis of the Church's order is, as we have said, founded upon the bishop's authority. The layman has no right of protest. For him the papal decree is binding; it is the word of God. If the laity cannot accept the Church's discipline, then it has no right to accept its blessings. The Catholic woman may feel her gorge rise in disgust at the inhumanity of denying her the ability to control her body, but she cannot deny the Church's right to do so. If she feels that life, even with the Pill, would be unbearable without the comfort of a periodically murmured absolution through the chink of the confessional, then she should not protest. After all, not so long ago the Holy Father would have ordered her man and sons to fight for the Church against the Saracens in some far-off land.

The heartbroken wives and mothers could not then go before television cameras and bewail their disillusionment with Mother Church, more interested in saving her estates than men's souls.

The lesson of all this anguish for the world is that religious principles are not necessarily humanitarian in effect or intent. They are basically theological; not moral. We who are outside the Church have no right to criticize the decisions of the hierarchy in such matters as the Pill, for the assumptions on which their logic rests are irrational, religious. We would rule differently because we should not start from the Church's premises. Ours is the much more difficult task of seeking solutions to the world's problems as they arise, each on its own merits. We avoid the blind application of general principles knowing full well that most human problems cannot be so resolved; they present delicately poised alternatives far more often than clear cases of right and wrong, good and evil. A monolithic religious authority might feel itself justified in creating havoc and suffering in obedience to some divinely ordained precept. Lesser men must walk warily. We have to answer not to some remote deity in a vaguely defined after-life, but much more fearsomely to our fellow men in the present. We cannot sit back in our papal thrones and contemplate the ordered beauty of our palaces; we have to look into the eyes of those who say we have betrayed them when they most needed help. A religious morality may suit the Church: we need some more humane guide.

CHAPTER SIX

A Question of Perspective

FOR the Christian, as for many other religionists, life does not end with death. One of the strengths of this belief in the after-life is that it lifts man from the order of perishable flesh to that of the angels. As a son of God man cannot die, even though his body might rot away. The soul is imperishable and must return to its Maker. In *The Sacred Mushroom and the Cross* we saw how this idea of a continuity of existence is part of the fertility concept. The god's semen poured from the divine phallus into the labia of the earth's womb and settled in a great underground lake, a fount of wisdom and creativity. Man, like all living beings, has within him some measure of the god's seed, which cannot die, and when the flesh can no longer contain life this divine essence seeps back to the subterranean reservoir.

Furthermore, all creation needs heat, and the earth's uterus was aflame with this vital energy. This is hell-fire, and thus Pluto, the Greek god of Hades, was also the god of fertility and riches, as the newly discovered origin of his name clearly demonstrates. Later theologians saw the fiery furnace of the underworld not so much as the place of cleansing the soul of dross before rebirth, as a punishment inflicted upon it for wrongs committed on earth. In this way they succeeded in providing religion with its greatest incentive to doing good, or at least abstaining from evil, but it made nonsense of the idea of a continuing cycle of creativity. If the erring soul is doomed to an eternal roasting, it cannot be reborn. In this sense, the Buddhist doctrine of reincarnation remains truer to the old philosophies than the Christian.

On the other side of picture, the Christian believes that the soul, released from its mortal cage, flies aloft to see the face of God. The earliest Christians brought this experience forward by subjecting their bodies to various disciplines and drugs which, in their eyes, temporarily gave the soul a freedom from the body which enabled it to reach the seventh heaven and learn the secrets of the deity. So thrilling was this encounter, so glorious the visions opened up to the subject, that he wanted only to con-continue in that blissful state. He felt that could he but rid him-self of the cloying flesh and sensual appetites that kept him bound to mortality, he might for ever behold the face of his Father in heaven, as Jesus says of the angels of 'little children'. It was 'sin' that held the believer from enjoying this mystic communion with God, and for the religionist that term encompasses far more than moral turpitude. 'Sin' in its proper, religious sense is rather a state than an act. It may arise through some immoral deed or word, but it can equally be brought about by a wrong attitude to God, a neglect of the Church's offices or spurning of her sacraments. As a peculiarly religious word it has no place in a secular vocabulary. The non-religionist may speak of immoral or unethical conduct in the sense that it adversely affects harmonious relationships with one's fellow man. When the priest speaks of 'sin' he means primarily something which obstructs the believer's communication with his god. It is a barrier to heaven.

The concept of eternal reward and punishment has, of course, no part in a secularist's moral outlook. For him how you live on earth and treat your fellows has to be looked at in terms of human life, not death. Justice has to work here or not at all. He cannot shrug his shoulders at social ills and murmur something comfort-ing about the final levelling, or every man getting his just deserts in the hereafter. It is true that many of the great social reformers of the past have been Christians, but in a sense they have been thinking and working in what their Church would consider a shrunken perspective. Others of their faith have felt no such claims upon their social consciences; it was enough for them that the downtrodden peasant or refugee should seek solace in the Church and promise of better things after death. The Church itself was more concerned to maintain the status quo; had not Saint Paul urged slaves to 'be obedient to your masters, with fear and trembling, in singleness of heart, as to Christ'? Whatever his task, the slave should 'work heartily, as serving the Lord not men, knowing that from the Lord you will receive the inheritance as your reward' (Ephesians 6^{5ff}, Colossians 3^{22ff}). To take upon himself the task of asserting even a slave's independence and dignity, and to try to correct and even forcibly overthrow the social order, the Christian reformer was in fact blurring the edges of the doctrine of heavenly reward.

Nowadays, proportionately less reformatory zeal stems from the Church; those who in earlier days have worked from within a religious organization to sponsor humanitarian causes find it often less restricting to claim no particular religious or denominational bias. Even the Salvation Army does not now always make a prayer and hymn a necessary prelude to soup and a wad. The larger charitable organizations like Oxfam and the Save the Children Fund would not only lose many of their supporters if they began to wear a specifically religious label, or even laid claim to a Christian idealism, but they would find themselves barred in many of the countries in which they at present operate so successfully. Nevertheless, this kind of non-religious social aid is by no means restricted in its outlook to the present time. Its workers may not look to heaven for the righting of wrongs and healing of wounds, or rest content to pray for the eternal damnation after death of those who inflict the suffering they try to relieve, but they do have a longer sense of perspective than the here and now. The secularist reformer of the present day, no less than the old fertility philosopher, sees a continuity of life which makes even his failures worthwhile. He works as much for future generations as he does for his own. The campaigner for equal status for coloured people in a white society may feel obstructed and frustrated by the unreasoning prejudice of those about him, but he knows that if he can build only a few tentative bridges among the young generation, their children may know more tolerance than their parents and far more than their grandparents.

Perhaps one of our greatest problems in a pagan society is maintaining the impetus of working and thinking to a long perspective. It is too easy to lose faith in the future when its existence seems to depend upon some politician with an itchy finger. Nevertheless, social progress is only possible when the reformers can look beyond their own generation. On a personal scale, living unselfishly within a community really only makes sense if one believes in the continuity of the social order. Commercial hotels in a busy town are probably the unfriendliest places in any country; their inhabitants are birds of passage, with little feeling of responsibility towards the person in the next room. On the other hand, there is a wealth of unselfishness and what is commonly labelled 'Christian' charity shown in the meanest city slum. The inhabitants have a mutual bond in their poverty and realize that they are committed to their communal life probably for their whole lives. In such circumstances living unselfishly is a necessity; it needs no high religious or philosophical reasoning to demonstrate its advantages. But if the town-planner comes round and promises the destruction of the whole area and the resettlement of its people in scattered 'model' estates in six months, will the communal spirit last out the period?

It is commonly said that the shadow of the atom bomb overhangs the youth of today and accounts in large measure for so much of their fecklessness; living to a purpose seems hardly possible if the future depends on the will of some madman in the Kremlin, the Pentagon or Whitehall. But it would be wrong to blame only the bomb and the fear of sudden death for this unwillingness to work for the future. The breakdown of the old religious belief in the hereafter is as responsible. Perspectives have become foreshortened. Even a normal lifespan is not enough to warrant the self-discipline required for unselfish living, let alone one threatened with sudden curtailment. As long as a young person could be convinced of the existence of heaven and hell, he could see an extension of his life beyond any activity on this plane which might, even subconsciously, affect the quality of his life and his relationships with other people. Now that the after-life is to many little more than a joke; heavenly bliss the product of manufacturers of cigarettes, perfumes, feminine undergarments and spring mattresses, and hell a mild expletive or a laddered stocking, the extent of social responsibility would seem limited to the seven or eight decades of a normal lifetime.

The old fertility cults pictured the rebirth of nature at springtime as the rising of the god from death. The worshippers of the sacred mushroom saw in the fungus a microcosm of nature; it rose from the womb or volva, flourished, and within hours had died again, to be renewed in the continuing cycle of creation. Thus the 'Jesus', born of the virgin womb, lifted high on a cross as a sign to men, killed and raised again to eternal life, became a personified enactment of the life cycle of the sacred mushroom, and to the Christian today, persuaded of the historicity of the myth, serves as the supreme example of God's creative and redemptive activity in the world.

The idea of the dying and rising god is not primarily a moral concept. It has basically nothing to do with heaven and hell and eternal rewards and punishment for acts committed on earth. Nevertheless, it does express a commonly observed reality of life, that the natural order of creation, death and re-creation is a continuing process, and that no single action or thought is ever completely independent of what has gone before or will come after. What we are as individuals depends largely on what our parents were, as our children's heritage must determine very largely their attitudes. We have a responsibility extending beyond our own lifespan; the thinking person's perspective cannot, therefore, be limited to his three-score years and ten. Furthermore, as in the natural world no plant or animal life can exist on its own and all rely to a greater or lesser degree on their environment and fellow-creatures, so humans also are interdependent and bear responsibility for one another. This is a clearly observable fact and needs no abstruse religious philosophy to demonstrate it. It is the basic principle of secularist morality, and is as comprehensible to the child at its mother's knee as the politicians at the United Nations assemblies.

In these terms, punishment and reward are self-generating. We create our own hell when we harm the other fellow, since we break the chain of inter-responsibility on which we all depend. We attain true happiness when we owe no moral debts and are at peace within ourselves. At those times we are in what the old natural philosophers would call a state of balance with our environment.

Of course this concept of self-imposed punishment does not obviate the need for external discipline. In some remote, ideal society one may suppose a state of affairs when all people are moral since their inner perceptions are so finely attuned to spiritual peace and disquiet that they rule their every thought and action whatever the temptation to take advantage of the weakness of their fellows. We are not there yet, and such is our evolutionary heritage and the strength of our instincts for self-preservation, we may never attain that blissful state without a radical change in our genetic structure. Until then we shall need on occasions to wield the big stick and generally to restrict the freedom of lawless members of our society. But in every case the aim of punishment must be to restore the balance which law-breaking disturbs. We are slowly coming to realize that simple revenge, whether inflicted by individuals or by the community, is no answer to crime. Some of the old religious concepts of a 'righteous' god consigning the sinner to perdition and hell-fire derived more from primitive ideas of vengeance than justice, and are still detectable in the cries from reactionary circles for viciously punitive measures in the sacred cause of 'law'n order'.

Hatred of the wrongdoer is as destructive as the harm he inflicts. Two wrongs do not make a right. In terms of the old fertility concept, to follow one blow by another, to hate one's enemy, is to increase the initial imbalance caused by the first wrong, not to correct it. That was the failing of the primitive law-code which demanded an eye for an eye and a tooth for a tooth. It at least prevented over-reaction by the antagonists and an escalation of the feud, but in the hard reality of common practice the exactly judged retribution did not restore the balance. The two eyeless individuals did not thereafter love each other and live in peace; one-armed men can still bear and wield a sword. For the wrong that men do against each other is not to be measured in limbs lost or cattle stolen, and requital made in kind. The pride of the afflicted suffers often as much as his physical faculties or pocket, and wounds of the mind demand a more effective balm than material compensation. Naked revenge brings only deeper bitterness on both sides, and the avenger's 'pound of flesh' is bought at the price of a warping of his own personality.

One of the great puzzles of the religious moralist has been why, in a world governed by a righteous deity, goodness is not automatically rewarded by prosperity, and evil-doing by destitution. It has been only too painfully obvious that the reverse is more often the case: the wicked prosper at the cost of the righteous. The Old Testament book of Job plays out this theme in dramatic dialogue, as Job sits bewailing his fate on his dunghill and demands to know why God has thus treated him when his moral inferiors go scot-free and prosper. The proposition of his 'comforters', that mere man has no business questioning the workings of the divine mind, merely destroys the whole concept of natural justice; man is but a pawn in the hands of a capricious deity, with no rights save to serve God blindly, trusting that somehow and somewhere he will be vindicated.

This is certainly not the answer of the fertility philosopher. There must be a sense of balance, or natural justice, in the universe or life could not continue. Wrongs there will always be, but they must eventually be countered by good or the whole system would fall out of equilibrium. Men will prey upon others, become rich at their expense, and becoming thus more powerful will open ever wider the rift between them. On the international plane, nations prey upon weaker peoples and use their resources to increase their own wealth and extend their influence over other lands. A great rift is opened up in humanity between the haves and the have-nots and the process is apparently self-generating. Even when wiser counsels prevail in the richer lands and wealth begins to flow back slowly into the vacuum, the immediate effect of a higher standard of living is an increase in population unmatched by a corresponding expansion of food production. Poverty becomes even more desperate and tension between rich and poor increases rather than decreases. We have reached such a state in the world today, when even humanitarianism in foreign aid from the richer countries has so far provided only means for deepening the rift and further upsetting the balance between population and resources. To withhold aid would be merely to quicken the process.

In terms of a fertility philosophy there can only be one end.

The balance must be righted; the greater the imbalance the more violent the restitution. Seeing the present world situation with eyes raised to a long perspective, a violent revolution which would make the Russian upheaval of 1917 look like a ripple on a mill-pond seems inevitable.

Jewish and Christian eschatology, the doctrines of the last things, have similarly forecast eventual catastrophes in the affairs of mankind. Their prophets of doom, seeing around them the results of man's cupidity and the inequitable division of wealth, spoke of the righteous God's direct intervention and disruption of the world order, followed by an imposed peace and thereafter direct theocratic control through His priests. Such a prospect has seemed a barren hope to those millions of unbelievers who were either to be swept away in the holocaust or to survive to be ruled over by an ecclesiastical hierarchy responsible only to their deity. The eschatology of the secularist is no less fearful in contemplation: violent revolution from the East and a world nuclear war, at the end of which the planet would barely support life in any form. But the end would not be determined in place or time by the will of an autocratic god, but by the working out of a logical sequence of events that are part of the whole creative process. The hope the secularist offers, however, is not the self-surrender of puny man to the divine caprice, but the possibility that by his foresight of events and appreciation of the nature of the forces at work in the universe, man can forestall the catastrophe that threatens him.

Here is the essential difference between the religionist's view of the future and the wide-perspective philosophy of the modern pagan. Both see all too clearly the dreadful possibility of man's self-extinction, but the religionist finds his only hope in submerging his will in God's and resignation to the inevitable. If the worst comes, at least he will go to heaven. The secularist dares to believe that he can control the future by making nature (or God) subservient to his will. He will be God and determine his own destiny. If he has the will, man can right the imbalance in human affairs and thus forestall violent revolution.

For the first time in history those same forces that have worked towards aggrandisement and self-destruction have brought a potential solution to the problem they have imposed. The vast expansion in knowledge and resources that modern technology now presents to mankind not only deepens the rift between privileged and under-privileged nations but makes its bridging possible. The United States of America has the ability of giving from her vast treasuries of natural wealth and technological expertise so lavishly to the under-developed nations that she could speedily transform their economic prospects and thereby reduce the voltage potential of revolution. What is more, she could do this, and still remain rich herself. She has untapped resources in her own continent that could replenish her coffers quicker than her technologists and educationalists could use them abroad to establish power plants, factories, schools and agricultural facilities. She could banish hunger and famine for ever from large parts of the globe, and create such new markets for industry that the latent energies of the emergent nations would be too fully and gainfully employed to be diverted into bloody revolution.

Never before in the story of human civilizations has the amassing of wealth by one nation been on such a scale as to enable it voluntarily to correct the imbalance brought about by its accumulation. If all the riches of Nineveh or Babylon were spread out over the lands overrun and pillaged by the Assyrians and Babylonians, or the wealth of the Pharaohs were divided among the peoples of Africa and Asia, or the caliphs' palaces in Baghdad stripped and their plundered spoil re-distributed throughout the lands of the Crescent, there would still have been hardly enough money to buy each peasant a loaf of bread. The great cities of the world would have been desolated and their merchant princes left scrabbling in the dust for food, but the general level of prosperity among the peoples of the world would scarcely have been affected. America could, if she so wished, lead a crusade of the richer nations against poverty that would enhance their own economic position as at the same time it lifted under-privileged peoples from their slough of hopelessness. She and they would still remain rich, but they would have filled that vacuum sufficiently to reduce the pressure towards a violent restitution of economic imbalance that is otherwise inevitable. Foreign aid on these dimensions would make everything so far done by America and the Western world look like the handout of one soup kitchen.

All this is possible, but at present reckoning, unlikely. There is in that great country a disillusionment and a tendency to draw back from world commitment. She is soured with war, and resentful at the way those who have lived on her aid for so long reject her overtures to friendship. Her ambassadors are reviled, even kidnapped, her planes hi-jacked, her tourists bled and despised. On a smaller scale, something of this rejection of responsibility for the under-privileged by the better-off can be seen in Britain today. The Welfare State, admirable in conception and still a model for other liberal countries, has brought with it a hardening of attitudes from those on whom the burden of its upkeep must fall most severely. A man who finds he is having to pay twice for the education and welfare of his family because he seeks a standard better than average, and at the same time sees his income continually reduced by increases in taxation, not unnaturally feels less inclined to respond to appeals for the homeless and the destitute.

It is easy, in the face of ingratitude, to throw up one's hands and relapse into self-interestedness. The family man has, after all, enough to concern him with his wife and children without spending his evenings running a lads' club. The United States has internal troubles more than enough to occupy her attention without raising taxes to pay for wars to protect other people's freedom, or to stock other people's larders. Yet her more enlightened statesmen know that to retract now will invite doom in the future.

The rich man cannot afford to neglect the homeless and destitute. If ever a right-wing government in Britain tried to reverse the trend towards fairer shares, to introduce a stricter means test, to offer relief to the poor only when they have, as it were, bowed the knee to authority and made public acknowledgement of their 'crime' of poverty, our country would suffer the disruption of society that so far we have mercifully avoided by common sense and 'fair play'.

At the individual's level, we cannot afford to live for ourselves and withdraw from consideration of our neighbours or of succeeding generations. A good father will provide for his family during his lifetime, and will make provision by insurance and savings for their welfare after his death. His concern for those he loves must derive from a long perspective which has nothing to do with heaven and hell. The withdrawal from the world practised by the religious mystic, the hippie and drop-out, is the antithesis of this attitude. Like the modern drug-addict, the original Christian with his 'Jesus'-fungus seeks instant heaven and a repudiation of his need for involvement in the affairs of those about him. He seeks a personal 'salvation' which is an essentially selfish pursuit. He renounces the long perspective and claims self-sufficiency. But a moment's consideration shows how false this claim really is. The religious mystic in his cell relies upon the generosity of his fellows to feed and clothe him, and to make his separation from the world physically possible. The hippie leaves his settlement to find jobbing work within the society he has repudiated. He builds his shack with rubbish from the same source, and even the 'pot' that he smokes is prepared for him by the callous machinations of big business.

If the world is to survive the next few decades it has to harness the discontent of its youth with the present inequitable order to an active involvement in life, not a repudiation of it. This means that they have to see their rôle as part of a continuing process. The trouble is that too often their idealism and discontent has been channelled into attempts to bring forward the very chaos which we must at all costs avoid, the overthrow of order and the establishment of economic balance in one immediate upheaval of society. On the university campus and in the streets they have proclaimed the gospel of fair shares for all; they have seen the vision of the new world, the goal of the fertility philosopher. But the natural impatience of the young has demanded its immediate implementation by force; they have foreshortened their perspective. They have confused the desirable end with the most undesirable means of achieving it.

The youthful rebel is falling into the trap of the religious eschatologist: the world is so wicked that God will have to intervene and sort things out anew. This 'Flood' mentality has been responsible for more misdirected effort and suffering than perhaps any other aspect of religious ideology. We still have Jehovah's Witnesses knocking at our doors promising the end of the world in a few years' time and gaining converts of fear. They and similar Christian sects have been doing this for two thousand years, each managing to find in the Scriptures 'proofs' of the date and place of the end, and all apparently quite undeterred by the stubborn refusal of the world, or God, to fulfil the previous predictions.

We can laugh at their stupidity and weep for those they mislead, but the eschatology of the revolutionary is no less shortsighted and dangerous. It seems to some convincing because the doctrine of the end, of a radical realignment of world forces through the over-aggrandizement of one society over another, has an element of truth. There is, as we have seen, a natural tendency of nature to reassert a balance, but the violent collapse envisaged by our religionists and political hot-heads would be an unmitigated disaster, not a blessing. Given the time and the will we can on our own volition bring about that necessary equilibrium, and the world could be for all a happier place. Let the mighty forces of nature or the radical mania of the religious or political salvationist do it for us violently, and mankind will almost overnight be back in the Stone Age. It is all a question of perspective.

CHAPTER SEVEN

Thinking for Oneself

WE have already suggested that the discrediting of the Church's authority as a purveyor of truth could have profound political consequences. Ever since the fourth century the Church has been actively engaged in politics, and although she no longer holds her vast estates by her own armies in the field, self-interest has traditionally ensured her support of the landowners over the peasantry. A belated attempt towards the end of the nineteenth century to warn the Vatican against too close alliances with unpopular right-wing régimes in Catholic countries had little success. Priest and landowner are still usually regarded as allies, where indeed they are not one and the same.

This political alignment has weakened the Church's influence in the emergent nations, sometimes to the point of provoking open hostility towards her ministrations by the authorities. In older countries like France and Italy, opposition to the church has polarized into strong anti-clerical communist parties finding their ideological affinities, though not necessarily political ties, with Russia. Over the years a kind of working agreement has been effected between the opposing parties, and in some places they content themselves with dominating their respective spheres of influence, avoiding continual open warfare and the division of family allegiances. This certainly makes for peace and efficiency in local government, even if it does not fulfil the promise of the Church's reputed Founder when he denies emphatically that he came to bring peace on earth, but rather division: 'father against son and son against father, mother against daughter and daughter against her mother' (Luke 12^{51-53}).

In other countries, however, where poverty is more rife and the division between landowner and serf wider, a more explosive situation exists. One thinks of the states of the southern continent of America where, since the time of the conquistadores, the Church has served as the right arm of the military governments. The sort of compromise arrangements seen in Europe are hardly possible here, and a new situation which suddenly undermines the Church's authority could have serious political and social repercussions. A wide dissemination of the news that for two thousand years Mother Church has deceived herself and her flocks about the nature of the Faith and the validity of her leaders' authority could well act as a catalyst to an already desperate situation. Where huge cathedrals stand cheek by jowl with the hovels of peasants who paid for them, and oppressive landowners have traditionally found their most fervent supporters among the clergy, there is likely to be little respect displayed by the laity towards a priest whose authority derives from a mushroom. In South America a peculiarly ironic twist lies in the fact that the priests who accompanied the Spanish conquerors to Mexico found already installed in the land a mushroom cult very similar, if not actually related, to the one which inspired the original 'Christianity'. Early Spanish chroniclers wrote in detail of the pagan Aztec cult which revered the diabolical *teonanacatl* ('food of the gods'), mushrooms which were eaten ceremonially for divination, prophecy and worship.

Without the moral support of a discredited Church, right-wing governments would find it even more difficult to control their extremist opposition groups. Furthermore, revolutions which might, for instance, begin with the forcible seizure of Church properties, would have a tendency to spread like wildfire to neighbouring countries where the sign of the Cross has been rightly or wrongly associated with exploitation of the underprivileged. The trouble with loyalties that are based upon irrational emotions like religion, is that they can be transferred to an opposing cause with as much vehemence as once they displayed to the first. The Church has probably no greater potential enemy in her midst than the really fanatical religionist. A village parson will treat with extreme caution the ardent spinster who is never off her knees or out of the church, who is on every committee and runs everything, from the church bazaars to the local purity league. When the anonymous letters defaming his morals start flying, he will know where to look first. Our own country still lives with the havoc caused when Catholicism became discredited in the time of the dissolution of the monasteries, when the crucifix and the cowled monk were equal targets for the fanatical destructiveness of King Henry's soldiery.

A further complication would ensue in South America, where the right-wing governments have often enjoyed moral and financial support from the United States and the active help of the CIA, less from love of those in power than with the aim of holding in check the revolutionist, communist-inspired groups standing in the wings. The Americans might then find themselves torn between letting the rebels take over, or responding to the combined calls for help from her erstwhile client governments and a strong Catholic lobby in Congress. If she were not careful she could find herself engaging her largely Protestant people in a religious war on behalf of the Vatican. Of course this is hardly likely, but certainly a violent overthrow of the Church in a delicately-balanced political situation like that obtaining in a number of South American states would have repercussions far outside the immediate area and strain the patriotic loyalties and religious allegiances of mixed communities in the United States and Europe.

From the maelstrom a new pattern of power blocs might

emerge. The Communists would certainly seek political advantage from the Church's discomfiture and claim the allegiance of a new mass of disillusioned Catholics. Into the emotional vacuum they would pour their own religion, no less compelling or irrational than the Christianity it replaces. The Marxist mythology may have no more basis in history than the Jesus-legend, but for those who are swayed by the dialectic of Communism, caught up in the fervour of its idealism and have seen the vision of the new world founded upon selfless endeavour for the common good, it has seemed to offer a more effective instrument for social justice than a capitalist-aligned Church. It is only when the new 'priesthood' has taken over and clamped its chains of doctrine and discipline more harshly than even the Church upon its converts that they awaken to the realization that they have merely exchanged one mental prison for another, and that the new hierarchy will suffer even less open debate and criticism than the Vatican. Even the land they wrested from the priests will be taken from them and absorbed into a commune to feed their new masters.

Need people go on being shuffled from one irrationality to another? Why is it that we are so easily persuaded to abandon the one faculty that raises us above animals, our powers of reason and criticism? How can even highly intelligent people cheerfully divide their minds into two quite separate compartments? One finds it difficult to understand how a scientist, accustomed to examining minutely every scrap of evidence that is presented to him in quest of some fresh discovery, can on a Sunday mentally prostrate himself before a priest who can hardly put two sentences together, listen to his platitudes and specious reasoning for highly implausible historical conjectures, and even accept his dictates about when he should sleep with his wife and how many children he can have. Presumably he finds it a welcome relaxation to be able to delegate responsibility in matters of faith and conduct to an authority which he need not question. Accustomed in his professional activity to tear to pieces every assumption, to accept nothing without proof, he is ready to come home and rest his critical faculties in those spheres where he can presuppose a fund of special knowledge not vouchsafed to him as a layman but through divine providence revealed to intellectual 'babes and sucklings'.

Yet such an explanation hardly covers another kind of intelligent Catholic, often a convert to the Faith, who reads widely and thinks deeply about both the theological precepts of Catholicism and its historical assumptions. He is often indeed far better informed on these matters than his priest. How, one might ask, did such a person come to accept a chain of reasoning which requires at some point a step into the dark of irrational acquiescence? You cannot argue yourself logically into Christianity, or indeed into any religious faith. There must come a stage when the seeker has to say, 'I do not know; I can but believe.' For most people the threshold is very low, and little mental effort is exerted beyond drawing pictures of Moses in the bullrushes in Sunday School, or helping Mother to make the white confirmation dress and remembering the required responses. But for the person who requires some rational justification for suffering hard pew benches, murderous draughts and stiff collars each Sunday, and ever more strident claims on his time and purse to maintain the Church's establishment, that threshold of blind acceptance must be high. Furthermore, like any scientist willing to step into the dark and assume a natural law before working back experimentally to determine its validity, the believer has to convince himself that otherwise inexplicable phenomena are best accounted for by the existence of a personal deity, or an invisible force in the universe influencing the mind and actions of otherwise autonomous individuals.

But the Christian has to go much further than this. He has to believe a whole series of propositions about the nature of that deity, of his moral purpose in creation, of his self-revelation in mortal form, of the particular historical circumstances of that incarnation and the abandonment of the otherwise immutable laws of nature in 'miracles', particularly in the restoration to life of a corpse. For the Catholic there is even more to digest concerning the authority of the Pope, his ability to speak in certain circumstances with the voice of God, and the delegation of special powers to his bishops and priests which allows them to forgive sins and to decide questions of morals and the most intimate sexual relationships between husband and wife. Where in all this is the threshold of blind belief for the thinking Christian?

The same kind of question might be directed towards the ardent Communist. Here, too, at some stage the intelligent party worker must have made a step into irrationality. The non-believer finds himself listening with growing amazement to the dialectics of the Marxist, as vast assumptions follow each other in quick succession, each unproved and unprovable, with conclusions which send chills of apprehension down the spine of anyone with any feeling at all for basic human rights.

Is it too much to hope that we can teach our young people to think for themselves, and think critically? One of the saving graces of this age of turmoil is that the intelligent youth of today is far more ready to question and criticize than his counterpart a generation ago. This may be difficult to believe at times when the university campus rings to a monotonous repetition of a single phrase from a thousand young throats, as if its constant refrain will open the gates to a new world. But those phrases are soon discarded for others, and the deposed philosophies as vehemently castigated in the coffee bars and lecture rooms as they had been earlier promulgated. New prophets with even longer hair and dirtier jeans announce the imminent arrival of the new era, and are replaced by others before even the promised dawn has had a chance to break.

Out of all this cacophony there emerges a constant plaint of disenchantment with the established order and a longing for a more equitable dispensation. This is no bad thing of itself. It offers at least an attitude of radical criticism which may make it more difficult for specious new philosophies to find permanent converts. We grow too easily accustomed to the idea that what we have always had is necessarily the best. It often needs a fresh young eye to discern the fallacies in our thinking, and to approach our problems from standpoints outside the normal range of our conventional approach.

Of course, not all the themes we hear thundered from the soap-boxes nowadays are new. Most of them are the same old rubbish about the solidarity of the working classes struggling against the reactionary forces of the hard-hearted capitalist, and the need to destroy government because any form of control means the exploitation of the poor by the rich, larded nowadays with suitable invective against the white racialist asserting his dominance over the black (racialist), and so on. The same old fallacies scream aloud and their rebuttal is drowned in the din of emotionalism and the jack-boot, mingled these days with the crash of exploding petrol bombs and tear-gas canisters. Nevertheless, the battered but exultant rebels regroup to re-think. Their next charge on the Dean's house is quite likely to be under a different banner. Behind all the silliness and extravagant claims and counter-claims, there is a seriousness of purpose and a depth of thought that would have served the youth of pre-war days rather better than some of the fecklessness and waste that then marked university life.

Can it save them, and us, from domination by one political extreme or the other? Surely the answer lies very largely with those who formulate our educational policies. For the question really is, are we going to teach our children to think for themselves, or demand that they absorb facts and ready-made attitudes mainly in order to regurgitate them later in an examination room? The danger is that the requirements of a technological society on school and college syllabuses are leaving less and less time for teachers to encourage students to ask why and how certain conclusions are reached. Those examinations which consist of alternative propositions requiring a simple assent or dissent are becoming all too common, but should be an anathema to any self-respecting teacher. They make for ease of marking, but what do they assess? Memory? Luck? Hardly rational thought and the ability to form critical judgements.

Certainly it must be acknowledged that at the primary levels of education assimilation of facts is a necessary prelude to developing the critical faculty. They are the tools of the trade. But increasing pressures on teachers' time and classroom space may make the 'tools' ends in themselves, and this, particularly in the realm of higher learning, must be resisted. In the first place there are few if any disciplines which can lay claim to a body of established, immutable 'fact' which, once learnt, need never be questioned. The 'tools' are but working hypotheses; the task of the university teacher is not least to show his students how to take them to pieces.

A sound educational policy designed to make young people thinkers and not mental 'sponges' will go some way certainly to ensuring their resistance to the extremes of irrationality in politics or religion, but it is not the complete answer by any means. In both spheres we see highly intelligent men and women accepting blindly the most extraordinary propositions which would not for a moment stand up to critical examination. The reason they do so can only be that they want to: that is, emotional volition overcomes their rationality. We are none of us computers, and logical reasoning plays only a minor part in most of our day-to-day decisions. We are governed far more by habit and emotion than deliberate calculation. Furthermore, in political and religious matters we are more likely to be swayed by our hopes for the ultimate outcome of our belief and actions than in the logical validity of intermediate reasoning. The religionist seeks a mystical union with his god since by that means he can influence the deity to give him what he wants most: rain for his crops, young for his women or animals, or the peace of assurance of sins forgiven and the power to resist temptation. The political visionary sees a new world of an ordered society in which individuals are free to develop their own potentional abilities to serve the common good. Both see and feel a compulsive need and are tempted to drive for the goal without tracing the logicality of each step. The religionist wants to feel the comfort of a God who cares for him and a peace of mind. In the realization of his own inadequacy he will suspend his rational judgement and believe in the supernatural, aware that he is trusting in the existence of something incapable of scientific demonstration. The political revolutionary, fully aware of the slow processes of social development, and of the inborn resistance to change in human nature, yet will convince himself that Utopia can be made overnight, and that the disruption of public order will suddenly release a fount of human goodness and self-sacrifice that will bridge the barriers of class, creed and colour and bring immediately the new egalitarian society of which he dreams.

It may seem harsh to relate the activities of the political revolutionary with the spiritual aspirations of the religionist, but experience has shown only too painfully that the latter's self-conviction of his god's favour can lead to his assumption of powers over his fellow men no less damaging to the human personality than the State's concentration camps. At least the politician has eventually to judge the rightness of his actions by the economist's graphs and the balance of payments. The religious leader seeks the approval only of his god and his 'voices'. The mental and physical anguish his decrees may inflict are but part of the discipline that brings the sufferer nearer God. After all, did not God make himself mortal to die in agony on the Cross – proof, surely, that suffering is at the heart of the universe, and ample justification for believing that it is the way to heaven.

The kind of specious reasoning that is used by politicians and priests to justify the need for (other people's) pain can be countered by rational thought, and we should lose no opportunity to train young people to exercise it. Of even greater importance is the need to teach them and ourselves the desirability of maintaining a balance between idealism and practicality. Both are essential to the good life, but if one rides roughshod over the other, the outcome is disillusionment and a tragic waste of good intentions, or a barren, soul-less concrete and tarmac jungle that is, in effect, a vast mad-house. Surely we can build a kind of Utopia, achieving a stable society based upon an equitable distribution of the world's goods, without bloody revolution. We can, as we saw, even now stave off the fearful catastrophe which threatens us through a growing imbalance between rich and poor nations by a voluntary redistribution of wealth. Cannot part at least of the religionist's longing for peace of mind and a sense of inner fulfilment be achieved through this same balance between idealism and practicality? Is not a man more likely to find this blessed state from his own creative activity in his home or society than on his knees by his bedside, or laying bare a tormented soul before a screen in the confessional? At least, helping his children do their homework, or his wife strip wallpaper, or his village run a youth club, is likely to teach him more about his own inadequacies, the need for humility and taking the long view of life, than conjuring up visions of himself roasting in hell or being patted on the head by Saint Peter at the pearly gates.

Furthermore, the world is now moving fast towards a new

technological era when problems are being posed with which none of the old political slogans or religious sanctions can adequately deal. Leaving aside for the moment the global need for economic equilibrium, in the advanced societies new situations hardly dreamt of a generation ago have to be faced within the next decade. No longer shall we be struggling to find work for an army of unemployed, that they may feed their families. It will be more economic to feed them and their dependants and pay the workers to keep away from factories that virtually run themselves. Already, some automobile operatives in America are given three, even six months holiday a year on full pay because their machines do not need them. In such a society the workers' symbol of hammer and sickle would be better replaced with fishing rod and shooting stick. Is this the revolutionary's Utopia? Surely not; work is the means, not the end, and the use of leisure and the development of latent talents to fulfil other needs than merely earning enough to live is fast becoming a major call upon our ingenuity and resources. Such a situation makes nonsense of the jargon of political extremism, and the Christian charity worker will spend more time looking for the poor than giving them soup.

The dangers that confront the over-leisured society are of the mind. People who have been taught properly will know how to think for themselves and need no pressing to explore fresh fields of learning and experience opened up to them by their new-found freedom. Those whose early training has simply provided them with facts to make them more efficient stenographers, car-washers, accountants, or (if they need facts) advertising executives, will find their only interest in life in comparing the relative comfort of psychiatrists' couches and the colours of their ceilings.

There is, however, another side of the coin. Can a society whose efficient administration depends largely upon conformity afford to be composed of people thinking for themselves? From an administrator's point of view, the beauty of the Catholic Church and world communism is that the laity is not supposed to think for itself, at least to an extent that leads it to question dogma. The present storm within Catholicism when editors of Church newspapers advocate views at variance with those of the hierarchy, and priests openly dispute with their bishops and receive the support of their congregations, strikes, as we have seen, at the very basis of Church authoritarianism. It is tantamount to arguing with God. Similarly the divisions within the Communist world are equally disturbing and heretical, and have no part in totalitarian ideology.

Nearer home, would Parliamentary democracy be possible if the House of Commons were filled with six hundred-odd members thinking for themselves? How could any government be confident of its powers to rule if it really had to persuade each of its ostensible supporters of the rightness of its every action? Of course, in the end the Cabinet has to take note of pressure groups within its own party and even change its policy to avoid open conflict. But on the whole, the prime ministers of our governments have wide freedom of action and can count on their majorities faithfully trooping through the voting lobbies at the ring of their master's bell and the crack of the Whip. The party system itself depends upon a grouping of interests, the workers supporting the Labour candidates at general elections, professionals and businessmen as blindly following the blue and white rosette and middle class accent. But what would happen if, with their increased leisure, the majority of voters were to begin weighing up all the issues, to size up the intellectual capacity of their candidates, give or withhold support only after asking questions about education, foreign policy, soil and water conservation, attitudes to abortion, birth control, state-licensed brothels, and so on? There is little sign of such a contingency at present, but it is true that the old party loyalties are gradually breaking down with an increasingly affluent society. Even the humble factory worker is becoming able to earn himself a stake in industry, taking up shares in his company's bonus schemes or buying unit trusts. He is becoming less susceptible to party demands for the nationalization of industries in which he receives a half-yearly share in the profits, or whose shares he hopes to sell on the stock market for a handsome profit. There may conceivably come a time when he will resist the call to strike because any advance in his wages that the shop stewards might wring from the management could reduce the company's potential to compete in overseas markets and thus their profit margins and his dividend. Similarly, there may come a time when the company directors, the professionals and shopkeepers will view a swing towards the right in the party of their traditional choice with consternation, and become fearful of supporting a government that in the sacred cause of efficiency will seek to erode the freedoms of the individual.

Ideally, the political parties should be based not on the grouping of class or professional interests, but on a consensus of opinion on key moral issues of government. And since this should derive from persuasion on a rational and not emotional level, cutting across sectional self-interests, it must depend upon a thinking electorate. Some of the biggest issues we shall have to face in the next few years are moral problems, and on the clarity and far-sightedness of our thinking and decisions will depend the future of mankind. It is just here that we have so far failed dismally to meet our obligations. A vital problem of ethics in the House of Commons is customarily thrown open to debate and the party whips withdrawn. At this point too often the honourable members melt away to their clubs and their Westminster flats and wait for the issue to have blown over. The members left to debate and vote upon matters like homosexuality, divorce reform, abortion, and the like are scandalously small. But after all, what can a loyal Socialist, put up by his trade union to speak for the interests of higher wages for car-washers, be expected to do when asked whether he favours legalizing 'pot'? How should a true-blue Tory sponsored by the City answer the proposition that organs should normally be removable from the dead (or nearly dead) for transplanting?

These are important and controversial issues, but they are simple compared with the kinds of questions that will soon be facing us. Already the old religious sanctions have been left behind. A Catholicism which is still restricted by a philosophy stemming from the idea that God is a mighty penis, his spermatozoa the rain, and the earth a vast womb, is hardly in a position to offer guidance to the rest of the world about euthanasia, artificial insemination of humans, the creation of life outside the womb, chemical control of personality, voluntary and compulsory eugenics, sterilization and abortion, and so on. The Protestant churches are in no better state to help, although their leaders are in theory less rigidly bound by traditional theology. In the British Upper Chamber there are a few occasions when a handful of the bishops can be dragged protesting from their dioceses to cast their vote against Sunday football or some other burning moral issue. Faced with something vital for the wellbeing of the community, the more vociferous can usually be counted on to oppose any real advance, the more radical thinker will cancel out the other's vote, and the laity will be left just as confused and leaderless as before.

In the larger issues that must soon confront us, the churches are out of their depth. A new situation has arisen when the world of technology is fast outstripping our powers to control the possibilities for good and ill it offers. In the days when we stood at a child's bedside and watched it die of diphtheria, there was nothing else to do but pray. If God so willed, the child lived; if not, he died. With the parson's help we simply had to come to terms with God. Now we can not only prevent the child dying of that disease and many others, we can almost prevent anyone dying of anything. At least, we are now able to stave off death from old people to the extent that the overcrowding of geriatric wards with the senile aged is fast becoming a major social problem. Glib axioms like 'reverence for life' are coming to have less and less relevance, and the Church's insistence on the ultimate value of human life, once a major factor in humanitarianism, is fast becoming a positive menace to the balance of populations in a number of countries.

We have urgently to rethink many of the old bases of western morality. As we can control more and more of our lives and need leave less and less to chance or 'God' to determine for us, we need to formulate new laws on an international basis. This cannot be done by clinging to the law-code of semi-nomadic Semitic communities, supposedly roaming around the deserts of north Arabia some three and a half millennia ago, nor even to its interpretation through the medium of a drug-cult of the first century. Many aspects of such tribal mores might still be valid, and will figure prominently in any new ethical system that may be devised. In that case it will not be because they form part of any religious revelation, but because their general effect on human relationships in the past has been seen to be good, and as far as we can see, may continue to be so. In so far as they reflect the belief of the old philosophers that there must be a balance in human as in agricultural affairs, they will serve as useful guidelines. But the vital issues that confront us today and will do so with even more urgency in the next few years will not be resolved by such vague generalizations nor, indeed, by looking wistfully back into the past to when God made our gravest decisions for us. From now on it is we who have to sever the cords of life, as it is even now we who decide when it shall be created. It will soon be we who decide whether the baby is to be a boy or a girl, be right or left-handed, be an intellectual or a craftsman, and so on.

Such decisions need a degree of self-confidence, perhaps even ruthlessness, which is terrifying to contemplate, but nevertheless has to be faced by society as a whole if we are not going to let our technology run away with humanity. We have to take courage, and think for ourselves.

CHAPTER EIGHT

Playing God

PERHAPS the cruellest dilemmas which civilized man has to face concern the taking of human life. On the battlefield, fear and mass hysteria to a large degree relieve the individual of the necessity for making rational decisions about whether his opponent shall live or die; if it's not the other chap, it's me. Even the general, secure in his headquarters, can calmly and methodically plan the extermination of hundreds and thousands of the enemy. He is the servant of his political masters, and has assigned the responsibility for the destruction he contemplates to the 'Government'. The politicians, even more secure in their Cabinet rooms, are but spokesmen and executors for the millions that put them in power. Responsibility for ending human life is thus distributed over the community, and guilt is a rare emotion in such circumstances.

Similarly, in those communities which still inflict the death sentence upon their criminals, responsibility for the judicial murder rests upon society as a whole and neither the judge nor the executioner need take the fearful act upon their consciences. Nevertheless, in war and in capital punishment society decrees that certain human beings should not live. A definite decision is made, jointly or individually, that in the interests of the community as a whole the lives of certain people should be forfeit. The Church has never found itself able to take an unequivocal line on either war or capital punishment. With such a bloody history behind it, it is difficult to see how the Church could do so. Does not the Master promise in the New Testament to 'cast fire upon the earth' (Luke 12^{49}), and urge his humble fishermen disciples in the story to equip themselves with swords (Luke 22^{36})?

Some branches of Christianity, placing more emphasis upon those reputed sayings of Jesus which command his followers to love their enemies, have preached pacifism. The Quakers in particular have sent the flower of their youth upon the battle-field, resolutely refusing to carry arms but bearing stretchers under the protection of their country's shells and mortars. Short of removing oneself entirely from civilization and living on some far desert island, it is difficult to see how a pacifist can entirely escape involvement in a war being waged on his behalf by his fellow-countrymen. In any case, 'loving one's enemies' can be variously interpreted. No doubt the executioners of the Inquisition were sincere in their belief that in destroying the mortal flesh of the heretic, they were demonstrating their love for his soul. Better to roast in the market-place at the hands of the Church than in hell in the company of the devil.

As a general rule of conduct, the sixth commandment may seem admirable. As a specific guide to the morality of taking life in judicial executions, war and medical practice, it is virtually useless. Indeed it has perhaps done more to cloud the vital issues raised by problems of life and death than it was ever worth as a general precept. As with any other written law, to be at all useful as a code of conduct it requires qualification and relating to specific cases. Merely to raise the sixth commandment aloft and brandish it as a divine prohibition of war, or abortion, or euthenasia, or suicide, or the like, is meaningless, not least because not everyone subscribes to the divine authority of the book of Exodus. In any case, one might reasonably have expected more than two Hebrew words to cover the whole human dilemma of deliberately taking life.

We are having these days to think about this problem ever

more urgently, and somehow we have to look at the issues involved unemotionally. Since the strongest instinct in animal life is for self-preservation, and for many the greatest fear is of death, to contemplate the taking of another person's life in cold blood seems beyond the capability of normal, rational human beings. Yet the problem has to be faced, and quickly. For mankind is fast reaching the stage where natural death can be held at bay by scientific means almost indefinitely. As we have said, our geriatric wards are already becoming filled with human 'cabbages', pathetic, senile human beings, kept alive physically by drugs, having to be waited on day and night by an army of medical attendants whose services are desperately required elsewhere in our hospitals. At the other end of the life scale, babies are being born hopelessly deformed physically and mentally who, a few years ago, would have died within minutes and are now being kept alive, even operated upon within hours of birth. Medical science is giving us power over life and death; what it is not giving us is the moral courage to use this power.

In days past, the good Lord took poor old Auntie Jane to his bosom after three score years and ten with a sharp attack of pneumonia. Again, in his wisdom he defeated the attempts of the midwife and doctor, when made, to save the deformed foetus. We mourned, but had through our tears to agree that it was probably for the best. Aunt Jane had lived well but there was nobody left to look after her properly, and she had been lonely since the death of Uncle Joe. The parents of the dead baby grieved their loss, whilst the mother wondered to herself how she could have coped with a cripple and cared adequately for the rest of the family, and the father mopped his brow with relief after the contemplation of what providing extra help and medical assistance might have done to a hard-pressed budget.

Now, Auntie Jane lives on, unwanted, seeing life through a haze of drugs, uncaring, unknowing. Her family come sometimes to see her and sit by her bedside, unrecognized, wondering when they might decently leave and breathe out the smell of death that hangs about the room. The doctors present to the baby's parents the product of weeks or months of intensive application of the most advanced medical techniques known to modern science, alive, its heart beating, its body for ever horribly deformed, and, for all the love and affection its mother may bestow upon it, for ever a burden and emotional strain upon the family.

Who shall make the decision that life is not worth saving? And having decided that life should end, who shall cut the thread, deliberately withhold drugs at the next bout of pneumonia, fail to clear the baby's lungs at birth? Such decisions have to be made, and stabbing angry fingers at the Ten Commandments will not resolve the problems. We have gained power through our technology and now have to learn how to use it. There is no going back. We cannot sit and yearn for the days when the good Lord gave and took away, and mankind sat helpless and hoped for the best. Decisions which we had previously left to chance or fate or God have now to be taken by ourselves, and the prospect makes cowards of us all. This is understandable; what is quite intolerable is that we should make others bear the burdens we shrink from undertaking.

'Of course,' we say to our doctors, 'you must not kill; but you do not have officiously to keep alive.' Translated into action this means, 'the next time the old lady develops a temperature make her as comfortable as possible and let her die'. But the withholding of drugs is as much a positive action as injecting an over-dose of morphine. At some point the doctor makes a conscious decision: the patient shall die. He dare not acknowledge that decision publicly, perhaps not even to himself, but he has nevertheless made it. Society knows it, grieves with the bereaved, and is untroubled. But murder has been committed on its behalf.

A thalidomide baby emerges from the womb, seen to be without arms or legs or otherwise horribly deformed, and is allowed to choke. The doctor or midwife who has not cleared its lungs could be accused of infanticide; a Roman Catholic nurse present at the time and outraged by the action could make trouble and the authorities would be required to take punitive action. Society might thereafter pride itself on its humanity in re-asserting the sixth commandment. Will the parents faced with the burden of a perpetual cripple draining away its mother's energies and straining the family ties be quite so self-congratulatory? But Society does not allow parents the right of deciding the fate of their own creation. A father knowing the probability of deformity, might plead with the doctor to destroy a baby at birth but the decision would have to rest entirely with the physician, for it would be upon him that the wrath of the law would fall should his action be discovered.

Most doctors, indeed, would refuse to comply with such a request. Their task, they would say, rightly, is to save life, not destroy it. Theirs is not to decide who shall live and who shall die, at least until they are given a clear mandate by the community to do so. Of course, in practice they are taking such decisions all the time, and have always done so. In many cases of terminal cancer, it must be very doubtful whether it was the disease that brought about actual death, or the pain-killing drugs that had to be administered in ever-increasing doses if the patient were not to suffer unduly. The doctor is fully aware that in such cases he is deliberately hastening death, however euphemistically he may describe the process to relatives. Who would question the motives or morality of the action?

Nevertheless, society has no right to ask a doctor to bear the moral burden of ending life. We are reaching the situation when we shall have to decide for ourselves to end life where it is no longer meaningful or where it imposes intolerable burdens upon others.

The doctor has a right to demand clear and unequivocal guidance from Society. We can no longer shelter from our responsibilities under the cloak of piety or euphemism, and put the doctor with his syringe in the place of God. If we acknowledge that the physician's training is simply to cure people of their mortal ills, then he should not be expected to give moral judgements. He should not be called upon to decide on any but medical grounds whether or not a woman should have an abortion, parents should be forced to accept a deformed child they feel unable to care for adequately, or Auntie Jane should continue indefinitely in her 'cabbage' existence.

We are in danger at present of substituting our doctors for our priests. The surgery is becoming a confessional. Many general practitioners resist this process, not least because pressure of time in a busy practice just will not allow them to listen to an hour's outpouring of a patient's personal woes and sins to win an aspirin absolution, when the waiting room is crammed with physically sick people. But there are others of the profession who are not averse to assuming the mantle of the spiritual counsellor, and who are quite prepared to preach their particular brand of moral piety. To such doctors questions of abortion and euthanasia are not to be answered on purely medical grounds; they will dispense ethical judgements along with their medicine, and if they owe their allegiance to some restrictive or puritanical religious sect, pity the patient.

Society has to come to grips with this problem of moral authority and decide just where the various responsibilities lie. Above all, it has to educate its members to acknowledge that each person has to make decisions for himself, and must bear the weight of their outcome. We all need help, some more than others, but the goal to which society should move is the freedom of the individual to run his own life. Education ought to be geared to that end, and one of the heartening aspects of today is the self-confidence of so many young people, and the way that under wise and inspiring leadership they will undertake quite demanding 'projects' in and out of school requiring a large measure of individual initiative. But if that is the aim of our training of the young, we ought also to recognize that the rôle of the moral legislator must decrease. Certainly where the wellbeing of the community is really at stake, there must be safeguards. The lame dogs of society have to be protected, and the rights of the under-privileged maintained. But in matters of personal morals there should be an ever decreasing place for State control and a greater dependence upon the good sense of the individual, otherwise no moral progress is possible and we shall never grow up.

Similarly, unless we are going to allow parents to decide for themselves what kind of family they want, and women to determine whether they become or remain pregnant, then Society is taking upon itself not only the rôles of priest and doctor but also father and bread-winner. In this case the influence of the State in the personal lives and decisions of its members must increase rather than decrease. Instead of merely providing the expertise and facilities for people to make their decisions to serve the best interests of all, the State is abrogating parental responsibility and must therefore be prepared to supply the family's needs almost entirely from the cradle to the grave. This is indeed a very real danger at the present time with our Welfare State. With the lessening of the clergy's influence over people's lives, there is an army of sociologists, welfare workers, amateur and professional psychiatrists, and the like, pressing forward to take the Church's place. We are being flooded with reports of social conditions, committees to study the reports, and reports of the committees set up to study the reports. Making other people's minds up for them is a flourishing industry. There is now almost a vested interest in promoting personal inadequacy. We shall end up, if we are not careful, with more State-employed guardians of the young from the evils of drink, drug taking, and extra-marital pregnancies than there are drunkards, 'junkies' and unmarried mothers.

Recently, we in this country have at last had the courage to do something about the abortion scandal, although against much vocal and largely religious opposition. Legal abortion has been made easier, although much still depends upon the personal views of the doctors concerned so that there is wide disparity between the facilities made available in different parts of the country. Nevertheless, it is now more possible than it was before for a woman to seek help for the termination of a pregnancy when she and her husband feel that another child would make an already difficult situation virtually unbearable. A visitor from another planet might be astounded to learn that such a decision should in any case be anyone else's than the parents', and fail to understand why society, let alone an individual doctor, should be called upon to justify or otherwise an abortion requested by the progenitors.

Restrictions imposed by society on the termination of life, inside or outside the womb, have their origin in the age-old concept of the balance of nature. Life is the gift of the god and is thus sacred and inviolable. The god gives and he takes away, and to interfere with the natural process is a religious sin. If there are too many live births, the god will right matters with a plague or famine, or encourage men to make war and thus decimate the population. To spill seed or frustrate conception is thus a sin, as we have seen, and purposely to abort the womb or expose the child is a similar offence against heaven.

Where mankind had little or no control over the processes of nature, this religious sanction had much to justify it. But now that we are moving fast into a state of supremacy over our environment, we have to take upon ourselves responsibility for determining whether life shall or shall not continue. We teach our children that increased privileges bring greater responsibilities; if you are given pocket-money, it is up to you to make it last a week.

Now we have to teach ourselves the same lesson. If we are able to create more and more wealth, we have to learn voluntarily to share it with others less fortunately placed. If we can prevent babies from dying at birth or soon after, we have either to restrict conception or make food and space available for them to live. If we can keep old people physically alive well into senility, we have to decide when organic life has outlived its usefulness. We have, in other words, to learn to distinguish between human life as merely the functioning of cells and organs within the body, and life which is meaningful existence.

The difficulty comes, of course, in defining the word 'meaningful' – to whom: to the subject, his relatives, the community? The facile answer for the religionist is, 'to God'. All human life is sacred, for all people are the children of God. It is not for mere man, therefore, to place the value of one person over another; in God's sight all men are equal. As a safeguard against the tyrant, this dictum is valuable provided everyone, especially the tyrant, will believe it. It is manifestly untrue that all men are of equal value to the community, but the hand of a self-appointed purger of the dross of mankind has sometimes been stayed awhile by reminding him that even the cheat, profligate, and liar is a son of God, and that the deity alone has the right to judge his children. The New Testament makes much of the joy felt in heaven over the repentance of the sinner, and one is left almost with the impression that the sower of wild oats who is prepared to come back home when he is penniless, cold and tired of eating pig's swill, is a better fellow than the brother who went on helping out on the farm.

Once we find ourselves in the position of having to make value judgements, as in the cases of the thalidomide baby and Auntie Jane, we are 'playing God', and where do we stop? The religionist may argue that Adolf Hitler was a child of God, but most of us would have wished the German generals' plot had met with better success. All of us would doubtless agree to and augment Ko-Ko's 'little list' of victims for the executioner's sword of Titipu and elsewhere. But where innocent life is concerned, the value and 'meaningfulness' of the subject cannot be measured in terms of wrongdoing, as with the criminal, but simply in usefulness or positive harm to the community weighed against the rights of the subject as a human being.

Here again, some clear and if possible unemotional thinking is required. We too easily assume that the rights of the individual must imply living as long as possible. It is customary for the British Sovereign to send a telegram to all old persons attaining their century, and dear Granny is besieged with kind friends and reporters enquiring the secret of longevity so that we may all follow in the path and similarly be honoured with a cable from the Palace. But for most of us, living to the age of a hundred would be welcome only if we could be sure of retaining our faculties, and the thought of droning and dribbling away a further decade or two, unwanted in a home for the senile, will hardly seem worth the telegram when it comes. There is a Euthanasia Society dedicated to promoting legislation that would allow people to affirm their wish to be put to death painlessly after a certain age, or should they become incapable of a rational life before that. One would have thought it was a harmless request, affecting no one but the person whose life is involved and those immediate relations whose wish would in any case be presumed to reflect that of the subject. But it is not an issue which can at present count on much political support. Yet if we are not able to determine the value of our own life and the point at which it should be terminated, how shall we ever have the courage to face decisions about other people?

Once we stop positing an intelligent, moral deity as the supreme arbiter of life, and assuming the existence of an afterlife where wrongdoing is punished and welldoing rewarded, our philosophical perspective, as we saw earlier, is brought down into the plane of mortal existence. Moral balance is achieved not in an individual life's span but in the continuing life of the community. Value judgements have to be made within the same perspective. In this sense it may be true, in the words of Caiaphas, that 'it is expedient for you that one man should die for the people, and that the whole nation should not perish' (John 11[50]). And if such sentiments understandably send a chill of recognition down our spines as the common manifesto of the political assassin, that kind of judgement on humanitarian grounds will be ever-increasingly demanded of us.

It is a wonderful thing that the spina bifida baby can be operated on within hours of birth and kept alive. But if it is going thereafter to be a permanent cripple, utterly dependent upon others at the cost of the wellbeing of a family, or consigned to a state institution for all its days, is the operation justified? Is it really a humane act to let the baby survive? In decreeing that every possible effort must be made to preserve its life are we really abrogating our responsibilities in the matter? Are we not running away from making a difficult moral decision, following a general principle of very dubious validity that all life is sacred and of equal worth? It could well be in such a case that society is doing real harm to the family concerned, and there have been instances where the parents have drifted apart under the strain of the mother having to lavish all her time and attention on the cripple at the expense of her husband and other children.

It may be argued that life cannot be a bed of roses for anyone, and that a calamity of this nature could conceivably have the opposite effect of drawing the parents ever closer together. It is true that the greatness of man is nowhere better demonstrated than in adversity, and that suffering can temper the steel of courage. Much depends upon the circumstances and nature of the persons concerned. In the case of the spina bifida or thalidomide baby, the parents may consider they have the courage and material resources to overcome whatever difficulties their guardianship of the child may present in the future. They may believe that science will, in the child's lifetime, find ways of giving it a better and fuller life than can at present be contemplated. But surely the decision should be theirs to make and the State should allow their judgement either way to be upheld. At the same time, the community has the right to make it clear that a decision to allow the baby to survive will commit the parents to its care. If we are to have the privilege of choice, we must bear the responsibility of living with our decisions. It would be the direst cruelty if the baby were to be nurtured into survival by the surgeon's skill and handed over to the parents, for them only to discover after a year or two that they were unable to care for it adequately, and had to return it to the State to live out its dearly-won life in an institution for the severely handicapped.

Similarly, if parents elect not to control their fertility by artificial methods and do not desist from intercourse, society cannot be expected to take over responsibility for the care of the unwanted children. We are daily presented by charitable organizations with harrowing stories of families living seven in a room in the poorer quarters of our great cities. Rightly we are concerned about such cases and ask how, in an affluent society, poverty like this should be allowed. Our natural sympathy is, however, somewhat checked when we realize that the family has been growing regularly by annual births, despite the impossible living conditions, and that their slender income, largely State derived, is expended not only in feeding the family but in contributing to the collecting box of the local priest who is doing his best to ensure that the fertility of the faithful church members is in no way diminished.

There is an obvious conflict of interests here. Certainly the State should not interfere too drastically in the rights of individuals to rear large families, where they have the means and will to provide for their children adequately. On the other hand, should the taxpayer be required to finance either irresponsibility on the part of a couple too indolent to take precautions against the birth of unwanted children, or to finance the results of religious doctrines which forbid contraception? Quite apart from the financial aspects of the matter, unwanted children born into a poverty-stricken family are likely to suffer malnutrition and serious defects in their upbringing and education. Has the community at large a responsibility for preventing this situation, as well as that freely acknowledged in civilized countries of seeing that once they are born they do not want for the necessities of life? If so, how far is society justified in making contraception obligatory in cases where further pregnancies will inevitably place further burdens on the community?

In countries like India, massive efforts have been made to persuade men and women, to be sterilized or to adopt easy methods of contraception, but with only limited success. Sexual customs, religious prohibition in Catholic-dominated areas, pride in fertility, and so on, have done much to counter measures to this end and balance out the ever-increasing live-birth rate and longevity of the population. In a democracy, forcible sterilization of males after an allotted number of live births from their wives would be abhorrent. But one must wonder, with the population explosion at its present rate, how long democracy in such countries can continue, and whether usurping totalitarian regimes will pay as much respect to the freedom of the individual to determine the size of his family, believing rather that the community's wellbeing must over-ride any more personal consideration in the emergency of over-population.

If man is going to 'play at God' in the sense that he holds death at bay at one end of the life span and refuses to control birth at the other, and at the same time checks disease and widespread plagues, he will be left with the last awful prerogative of the deity for keeping population in balance with the resources available: war. God could once always be sure that if one nation became too rich and powerful for the peace of mind and integrity of its neighbours, sooner or later they would band together to hammer Big Brother into submission, and as a result would succeed in decimating his and their own populations. Indeed, it might almost seem at times that man has built within him a propensity for trouble-making which goes quite beyond any instinct for self-preservation. Our comparatively affluent youth have never been so active in the streets, violently attacking anything or anybody in sight. For all their incantation of political slogans and affirmation of half-baked philosophies, much of their violence stems from a no more sophisticated cause than a need to assert oneself against the other fellow, and to inflict and suffer pain. It is as if a major war every twenty years or so were a necessary part of the natural order, and served as a natural device to check the growth of the human race.

One would hope that our 'playing God' could be effected in a more humane manner than anything displayed yet by the religionists' deity. But it is not inconceivable that in some dreadful '1984' situation, a top-level summit of the nuclear powers will be convened for the express purpose of starting a war that could reduce the human population of some parts of the planet to manageable proportions.

If the State has cause for taking steps to ensure that people behave responsibly in conceiving children, the same control may soon be required for seeing that we have a balanced population between the sexes. There is every prospect that within a few years a couple will be able to determine the sex of their child at or before conception. In those parts of the world where the birth of a son is traditionally a time for great rejoicing and paternal pride, whilst a baby girl is ignored if not actually exposed at birth, such power to regulate the sex of the foetus could lead to a dearth of females and threaten the continuance of the population.

In the western world, a father's choice would usually be for a boy, and the mother's for a girl, and one can foresee some undignified bedside squabbles about which hormone was to be administered at the appropriate moment. Certainly, if population statistics began to show a disturbing trend towards a preponderance of one sex or the other, some official action might have to be taken, be it no more than having a public relations firm persuade people that girls were 'in' and boys 'out' in one particular year. But it would be hardly less worrying if an overwhelmingly 'boy year' were followed by a similarly bumper 'girl year'. Could one depend upon the varying tastes of parents to even out the situation? If the possibility of determining the sex of one's child were offered parents, there can be little question that most would wish to make the matter one of choice rather than leave it to chance.

Here again, as with all questions of human beings 'playing God', the real problems are not so much in the exercise of power as in living with the results of our decisions. It is rather like building a house to one's own design. It is an amusing pastime to devise an ideal home. It becomes more exciting when the planning is for real, the architect has been engaged and the air is thick with grand schemes promptly laid low by the expert, re-formulated, adapted, squeezed into shape, and gradually translated into blueprint and bricks and mortar. The great day arrives, the furniture is moved in, and the proud owners take stock of their creation. Was that split-level lounge really such a good idea? Will the eighteen inch step down not need fencing if someone is not going to break a leg? Is the large plate-glass window in the bedroom going to give less a feeling of spaciousness and more one of appearing in a strip show for the benefit of the neighbours?

When Johnnie is exerting his masculine strength on the

priceless Dresden, or teenage Jennie is sobbing her heart out over the faithlessness of her first boyfriend, it will be a strong-minded Mum who does not regret, even for a fleeting moment, that she, or Dad, had won the battle that night and taken the pill from the other bottle.

A more subtle and vastly more dangerous ploy in the 'God game' may one day be possible. It is well known that surgery of the frontal lobes of the brain can profoundly change temperament. Some manic-depressive conditions have been considerably relieved by such operations where the doctors consider the permanent change thus effected in the mental outlook of the patient is on balance better than the previous state. Nevertheless it is not an operation that is undertaken lightly, and of late it has grown out of favour as less drastic and irreversible treatments by drugs have been made available to the neurologist. All the same, this growing ability to control mental aberrations by the use of surgery or drugs is one more important step in the exercise of power over the mind.

We all know of efforts made in this direction by intelligence agencies on spies and captured prisoners, ranging from mental bludgeoning during hours of interrogation to more subtle methods of interspersing acute mental and physical torture with periods of rest and simulated compassion. We are also aware of the so-called 'truth drugs' which render the subject less able to devise and maintain a self-consistent lie. It is now becoming possible to render the mind of an individual susceptible to suggestions and resistant to its normal emotive reactions on a far more permanent basis than that achieved by hypnotism or so-called 'brain-washing'. This power could of course be a wonderful boon to the doctor in curing manic-depressives and similarly disturbed people. It could also be extended to persons who are not really sick, but who have a tendency to become enraged over trivial things and very quickly lose their self-control. It might conceivably be used to render harmless those inmates of our prisons' security wings who, although not technically insane, are so possessed by a hatred of society that their release after however long a confinement would inevitably lead to fresh deeds of violence against their fellow men. Perhaps the use of such mind drugs might rescue juvenile delinquents from an almost inevitable lifetime of crime, and make them responsive to the normal disciplines of communal living.

Used over a much wider field, such drugs could give all men a levelness of temperament, avoiding the extremes of emotional imbalance that make our lives so often a burden to ourselves and our companions. This would be no different in principle, and probably safer in practice, than the present addiction to 'pep-pills' and tranquillizers, taken individually and often without medical advice. One can imagine a perfectly rational argument being adduced by wise men for a mass dosage of this 'equanimity drug' to induce in a whole population a mental attitude which would make policemen and soldiers almost unnecessary. We should all be law-abiding because none of us would ever be able to raise the emotional vigour to exert ourselves against the common weal. If the whole world were thus treated, war would be virtually impossible.

For the individualist, this is a revolting concept. But the wise man might argue that to remove by drugs the aggressive instincts of man that go beyond the need to ensure self-preservation does not imply that we should all be robots, devoid of all initiative, obeying only the will of our political masters. The temperamental behaviour often adopted by persons of artistic bent is often more a mark of their trade than strictly necessary to the exercise of creative activity. Some painters can bring masterpieces into being without dashing madly around a canvas on a bicycle daubing paint liberally on everything in sight. That most sublime act of creative beauty between man and woman, the sex act, can be performed and enjoyed by some couples without the extremes of violent passion found desirable by others.

In any case, it might be urged, few of us are or want to be action-artists. Most live out lives largely circumscribed by the nature of our professions and the daily needs of family life. Contrary to the impression given by authors and playwrights, such normal, undemonstrative lives are not necessarily dull. There is not under the skin of every bank clerk a James Bond screaming to be let out. For most people, outbursts of temper that come after a tiring day at the office, and leave the wife disgruntled and the children in tears or sullenly rebellious, are not the prelude to works of artistic genius. They more usually result in dyspepsia, a disturbed night and a sick headache the next morning. Emotional extremes in such lives would not be welcomed, and the happiest people seem to be those who can maintain an overall equanimity of temperament.

Even though mass dispensation of drugs of this kind might always be resisted, as even the beneficial fluoridization of drinking-water finds vehement vocal opposition in some places today, undoubtedly this ability to control temperament throughout one's entire life will be made more and more possible and generally available. If we want to live without extremes of emotion we shall be able to do so. Again, we are 'playing God' with our minds as certainly as the fool with his 'pot' and hard drugs. To whom are we answerable in this? Only to ourselves – or should we first consider those with whom we have most closely to live? A wife might consider a husband who never raised his voice, or could not be roused to heights of passion, a mere shadow of a man unworthy of her companionship. A firm might feel its executives and salesmen unfit for the task of leadership and marketing if they were too unemotional. The living theatre would die out and its devotees feel cheated of the high drama enacted vicariously on their behalf by the actors.

In summary, then, man as never before is being enabled to 'play God'. He has the prospect of controlling almost every aspect of his existence: he can create life when he wishes, and keep it in being almost indefinitely. He will soon be able to determine sex at conception, and to regulate artificially the temperament of himself and his fellows. He will manipulate ever more efficiently his environment to suit his own needs, and adapt his mind and body to fit the rôle his philosophers create for him in the universe. It remains to be seen if, while there is yet time, he can find in himself the self-discipline to wield this mighty power for the good of all. Having taken to himself the omnipotence of God, can he stand apart from himself to make decisions which he previously left to the deity? Above all, having taken those decisions, can he bear to live with the results?

CHAPTER NINE

All Things Bright and Beautiful

Art, like religion, appeals primarily to the senses. For many churchgoers the two are complementary. The majesty of a great cathedral, the tracery of a Gothic window and the splendour of its glass, the swelling of the organ and the clarity of a boy soprano can combine to make a deep emotional appeal which the worshipper readily identifies with religious experience. Artists have often in the past expressed their piety and sense of the grandeur and mystery of God through their creations on canvas, in stone and in music, and lesser men have thus been privileged to see heaven through their eyes. Even when the artist or composer uses the forms and symbolism of religious mythology to express his emotions, without necessarily acknowledging any particular religious belief, his work has still evoked a sense of the divine in the heart of the devout beholder. A gifted soprano singing 'I know that my Redeemer liveth' from Handel's *Messiah* need not be a pious Christian to awaken the religious sensibilities of the believing listener. Similarly, we do not need to be devotees of Venus or Dionysus to appreciate the exquisite form and symmetry of classic sculpture. Nevertheless, art and religion have always been closely related, and the portrayal of mythological figures as a common convention in the graphic and plastic arts has served to cement that relationship in the popular mind.

One result of this partnership has been to confuse the two, quite distinct, sources of aesthetic emotion. Art is not religion. They may be psychologically related and in worship complementary, but they are not synonymous. There are some people for whom the one passes into the other, in that they make art their god and devote their lives to his worship and adoration. But here we are merely confusing our vocabulary. God in the Christian sense is not a painting or piece of music to be reverenced as a supreme example of man's skill; He is a personality with a will of His own and with power to manipulate men's minds. Whilst certain religious rites may stimulate the aesthetic sensibilities of some people, this does not make them devotees of the god being thus served, nor does it necessarily put them into a state of intellectual submission to the doctrines of that religion or obedience to the cult's discipline. Many visitors to Greece have been entranced by the sights and sounds of an Orthodox service in a cathedral or humble Byzantine chapel without wishing for one moment to subscribe to that church's doctrines, or indeed enter into too close a relationship with her black-bearded clerics.

With the decline in religious observance, must there be a corresponding diminution of artistic inspiration and appreciation? We might, for instance, ask ourselves whether a lapsed believer can still obtain the same spiritual uplift from Handel's *Messiah* or Bach's *St Matthew Passion*. Many people, of course, lacking any religious belief, have never failed to appreciate such works, but it could conceivably be that those whose erstwhile piety is now to be matched by an equally intense revulsion from a religion they feel has failed them, may turn away from religiously inspired art forms as sour reminders of betrayal. Such a loss can only be temporary. The day will surely come when 'O Lamm Gottes, unschuldig, Am Stamm des Kreuzes geschlachtet' will move him no less to tears than in those days he suffered with his Lord through the anguish expressed in Bach's great chorale.

In some respects, the problems that confront us when we consciously separate art from religion are similar to those raised by the acknowledgement that morality and religion are not the same thing. We have to ensure that the one is not cast aside with the other. As we now have to seek new bases for our ethical standards and face the moral problems of a technological age without looking back to a 'biblical ideal', so our tastes in aesthetic appreciation must change and find new stimuli.

Perhaps our fault is that, in the face of a rapidly changing environment, we inevitably long for the past we understood and the artistic and moral monuments on which our own standards were founded. We are suffering just now in this country a rather sickening revival of 'Victoriana'; not because we are rediscovering beauty in what was by common consent one of the ugliest periods in British architectural and artistic history, but because it showed to the world a false front of solidity and unchangeability for which we yearn amid our shifting sands of uncertainty. Something similar lies behind our love for old churches, and even here and there encourages a revival of religious forms and sentiment. It would be a mistake to sink too much artistic and financial capital in rebuilding and propping up the past. A new technology needs, and is getting, new forms of artistic expression and architecture. A lot of it is probably undisciplined rubbish which will not last a decade, let alone a century or millennium. But it is doubtful whether we shall ever again build artistic monuments which will claim the admiration of the world a thousand years hence. Our equivalents of the French cathedrals whose building brought to their constructors grinding poverty for generations, are those monsters of gleaming alloy we shoot into space and eternity. The concentration of technological effort and resources their execution demands is the end in itself. Man has demonstrated his greatness; he has reassured himself that he is bigger than his environment. The medieval architects built magnificent churches to achieve the same sense of self-confidence. We construct rockets and send men on perilous journeys into space. Perhaps future generations faced with rebuilding Notre

Dame and finding new ways of propping up York Minster will bless us that having proved our point, we shot our creations out of sight and mind.

The adoration of what is past in religion and in art is a sign of failing nerve. It served our forefathers, we say, bringing them moral stability and aesthetic pleasure; it must surely do the same for us. In times of rapid change, as at present, nothing we create seems as stable as what is past. Religion has, it seems, to be rooted in antiquity to be valid. A century or so ago the Church was convinced that its written records of history extended back to the very creation of the world. Its theologians could thus trace the steady progress of man's thoughts about God from Adam and Eve to the final, glorious self-revelation of the deity in His Son Jesus Christ. Since there was no truth outside the Church, it could be confidently maintained that the answers to all man's problems could be discovered somewhere in its sacred literature.

It was not until the geologists and anthropologists began to show that the world was very old when Noah was supposed to have been riding out the Flood, and when archaeologists produced from the dust of Mesopotamia writings thousands of years older than the biblical traditions, that the Church's myth of sacred records coextensive with the lifespan of civilized man and the planet finally crumbled away. Nevertheless, for the average churchgoer, even in these days of television archaeology, the supposed time of Moses and even Jesus seems very far away. Time has lent the stories and teachings of the biblical characters a special authority; to be old is to be true. Small wonder then that in this time of swiftly changing fashions, of 'pop' music that is old in a week, new art forms which flourish for one exhibition and are forgotten by the next, the classics of music and the graphic arts seem imperishable by comparison. We forget that even the classics were once new and distrusted for their daring innovations.

As for religious teachings, we tend to overlook the fact that churches of all denominations are continually changing their interpretation of the Creed if not the words. There are fashions in theology as in any other forms of human thought. All insist on a biblical basis for their speculations, but their readings of the Bible vary from generation to generation. Some of the 'blood and thunder' theology of even fifty years ago, much of which still hangs on in gospel halls up and down the country, reads strangely to most modern churchmen, if only because the older clerics seemed so much surer of their beliefs and their scriptural authority than their present-day successors. If those lusty worshippers of the Lord we see in community hymn-singing sessions on Sunday television were to restrain their zeal momentarily and read the words of some of their best-loved hymns, they might be shocked. How many of those sweet old ladies, one wonders, really want their 'rest to be close to Thy bleeding side'? What beatific vision passes before their eyes when they describe in joyous harmony 'a fountain filled with blood, drawn from Immanuel's veins; and sinners plunged beneath that flood, lose all their guilty stains'?

We delude ourselves if we think to find an anchor for our beliefs and morals in Christianity merely because it is 'old'. In human evolutionary terms, the last two thousand years have been but a blink of the eyelid, and much of that time was a retrogression into the Stone Age compared with the cultural splendours of the centuries that preceded it. The Christian forms of liturgy and worship known to most churchpeople in our country are scarcely more than three centuries old, and even the Catholics are forsaking the ancient Latin Mass for a service in the vernacular.

Some Christian groups have been trying to break down this sham antiquity in the Church, and modernize its worship and moral outlook. They have sought to express their religious experiences in terms of the new art forms and beat music. Some have even looked to hallucinatory drugs to assist them in their mystical contemplations of the infinite. Knowing what we do now about the origins of the cult in the worship of the sacred fungus and the narcotic use of the drug it contains, this present phenomena is an interesting reversion to 'Christianity's' true nature. One can only hope that this unfortunate renaissance will be short-lived, and less harmful ways of stimulating the aesthetic sensitivity of the modern Christian will be found.

With the discrediting of the old historical assumptions about Christianity, the loss of the man Jesus from history, and the fresh doubts that must be cast upon the validity of the Church's traditional teaching on theology and morals, it may well be that the mystical or aesthetic aspects of church worship are all that remain to the Christian. For many of the younger members the old conventions of lofty spires, stained glass and traditional church music will seem irrelevant to the twentieth century, and more experiments in 'beat' or 'underground' liturgies and psychedelic extravaganza will make the headlines and shock the faithful. How long a laity for the most part committed to the glorification of the past will endure the innovations of the young is questionable. Even less likely to last is the willingness of the innovators to allow their imaginations to be confined within the conventions of organized religion, however loosely sympathetic clerics might be willing to define them. For, as we have said, art and religion are not one; the one must be unconfined in order to survive, whilst even the religious mystic seeks his vision within the discipline of ordered belief.

It is not difficult to foresee a breaking away of the more mystically inclined members of the Church to form in-groups dedicated to seeking together new spiritual experiences. For a while they may preserve the pretence of fostering religious worship, using the old symbolism and even liturgies, but without the discipline of the old order they reject, their mysticism will almost inevitably degenerate into individual sensation-hunting, comparable with the excesses of the Californian hippies. One significant difference may be that whereas pot-smoking is, one gathers, debilitating and anti-sexual, a concentrating of the faculties upon Christian symbolism, which is essentially sexual in nature, could lead to the kind of 'wild carousing' complained about in the New Testament as occurring in the 'love feast' (Jude 5[12]). Society might have reason for real concern if the Church youth clubs to which they have been sending their teenagers to 'keep them off the streets' reverted to the kind of 'Christian' behaviour which brought the loathing and fury of the authorities down upon early Church communities in the first century. Protected by the sacred symbol of the Cross, it is not easy to see what preventive measures Society could take to ban celebrations which their young participants could legitimately claim were more original activities of the Christian cult than anything purveyed by the normal worship of the Church. If the sign under which they gather represented both a copulating penis and vagina, and the fungus source of an aphrodisiac drug, one can hardly prevent people performing rites of religious worship that centre on the sex act and a god who was originally envisaged as a mighty phallus.

Eroticism can be an important constituent of the graphic arts as is evidenced particularly in Indian religions. It could well be that this deification of the sex urge might promote a revival of 'Christian' art in forms truer to its historical genius than the representations of sad-faced mothers with Michelin-tyre babies at their breast, or harrowing pictures of gaunt men being lifted down from a cross. However unwelcome such a movement might be to society as a whole, and the parents of the youth club members in particular, it would at least dispel the dangerously false notion that Christianity and morality are inseparable, and make us more ready to seek new foundations for our ethical values.

In whatever art forms religious mysticism may in the future choose to express itself, our communities will have the problem of deciding what to do with those monuments of a byegone piety that adorn or disfigure every town and village of our country. Some of the churches and cathedrals are sublime examples of the architects' and masons' art, and their loss through neglect and the death-watch beetle is not something a civilized society could tolerate. There are others, by far the majority, whose increasing sale for use as Bingo halls and boot-and-shoe warehouses seems admirably suited to their style of architecture. For such we need weep no tears, but only hope that economic considerations and the change in fashion for leisure pursuits will soon remove them entirely from our landscape.

The problem of safeguarding the really worthwhile relics of architectural and sculptural art is a very real one in any country proud of its artistic heritage. When those monuments are the responsibility of an ever-decreasing minority of the population, as is the case of the Church's places of worship, there comes a point where the community as a whole has to step in and share or take over the burden. Scarcely a week goes by without some fresh appeal for funds to save a cathedral from crumbling into dust, and the amounts of money involved become greater and greater. Nowadays, bishops and their staffs have to think in terms of millions of pounds, and aim their appeals primarily to industrial concerns who have any conceivable links with the cathedral cities. No longer can the provision of funds for restorative work be left to dwindling congregations or the collecting box at the door, left hopefully for the attention of the tourist. Even those vast financial thermometers so beloved of church fabric committees, which so effectively and hideously blot out from the beholder's camera the beauties he is being asked to help preserve, lose their paint long before they can register the optimistically placed boiling point of philanthropy.

On the other hand, the British taxpayer is averse to providing money to support the buildings of a religious order with which he has no spiritual or charitable sympathy. Why, he asks, should not the Anglican Church liquidate its vast City investments and sell its considerable lands to care for its own property? The situation is further bedevilled in this country by the fact that the Church of England is still part of the Establishment. Its nominal head is the Sovereign, who, with the Prime Minister of the day, appoints the bishops, who have a seat in the upper House of the legislature. On the other hand, the State is not responsible for the Church's finances and upkeep of its buildings. Clearly if some of our country's most beautiful architecture is to be saved from the ravages of time and heavy motor traffic, some clear demarcation of responsibility between Church and State has urgently to be decided.

In the end, however the money is found, the community will have to take over the upkeep and even administration of these buildings. When the Church reaches the point when it cannot muster sufficient clergy and congregations to mount its religious celebrations properly, we may wonder if the State will have to employ paid actors to stage the rites of the Church for their aesthetic appeal, a kind of perpetual Oberammergau for the benefit of tourists. Or will our churches become simply over-large and draughty museums, displaying to curious eyes relics of an age when Englishmen were persuaded in all good faith to worship a sacred mushroom?

CHAPTER TEN

Teaching our Children to be Good

NOT so long ago the only education many poor children received was in the village Sunday schools. Even today, some aspects of secular school instruction are religiously oriented, a relic of the days when a child's first reader was the Bible, and he knew the coastline of Palestine and positions of Jerusalem and Nazareth better than he knew the map of his own country and the whereabouts of the capital city. The Old Testament is still popularly regarded in many quarters as a primer of ancient history. Protagonists for compulsory religious education in our state schools often maintain that, quite apart from its supposed moral benefits, the children will learn much of the history of the ancient world. One of the most regrettable results of this well-meaning but misguided attempt to acquaint the young with religious ideas, has been to give an entirely false perspective to the study of human history. Children tend to come away from such studies with an astonishingly detailed knowledge of the names and dates of the kings of a small Semitic tribal confederacy between 1000 BC and 587 BC, and none at all of the major dynasties of Sumer, Accad, Persia, Greece and Rome.

Even supposing that the main course of Jewish history could be determined from the Old Testament, now even more doubtful as the result of our recent studies, to make this a focus of attention to the neglect or minimization of far more important ethnic and cultural movements is to throw all history out of focus. To maintain such teaching compulsorily in our secular schools in the vague hope that somehow our children will understand God's purpose in the world and this will make them good, has as much logic in it as the distribution on a massive scale of copies of translations of the Bible in the fond hope that they will convert some savages in far-off lands into good Anglicans. This kind of blanket coverage, whatever it may have done to fulfill the aims of the British and Foreign Bible Society, can only pay rapidly decreasing returns in the home educational field. Bible study in most classrooms is nothing but a joke. Head teachers experience more and more difficulty finding teachers among their staff willing to undergo the torture of trying to interest and keep the attention of a classroom of small boys in those parts of the Scriptures usually deemed suitable for their edification. The far more interesting passages in the Old Testament, dealing with the somewhat involved sex life of the main characters, feature only in the extra-curricular private study of the pupils and if anything detract from the book's supposed moral stimulus.

Too often religious teaching has been undertaken by teachers whose piety has outweighed their critical faculties. Stories of Adam and Eve and David and Goliath may do well enough for the average Sunday school, but placed in the context of secular education serve merely to discredit the teacher's objectivity, not to say veracity, in his instruction of other subjects. How can an intelligent twelve-year-old be expected to take seriously, say, a geography teacher's instruction in his own subject, when the next period he discourses with equal solemnity on the creation of the world in 4000 BC and the descent of the human race from a man and a woman in the garden of Eden?

Happily, it is not often now that the head teacher is forced to scrape the barrel to such an extent for his Bible instructors, and he will hope, faced with this burden of compulsory religious instruction, to find a member of his staff who will have taken some course of studies himself in biblical literature and history. Even so, that teacher has the unenviable task not only of maintaining interest in his subject among his critical pupils, but to try to put his instruction on the same objective level as is required for the other parts of the school's curriculum. He can, therefore, only use the Bible as a handbook for ancient history, perhaps as an introductory source for a study of ancient civilizations.

In order, however, for the teacher to be able to use the Old Testament for such a purpose, he has to acquaint his pupils with the rudiments of literary criticism. His class knows as well as he does, that the opening chapters of the book of Genesis are not what they purport to be, a true account of the creation of the world. The teacher has then to discuss the nature and purpose of mythology, and the position of the Old Testament within the corpus of other religious texts of the ancient Near East. Right at the outset, therefore, the teacher is placing the Bible on a level with other ancient sources and subjecting its narratives to the same kind of literary criticism as has to be levelled at extra-biblical materials.

The intelligent pupil is thus at once made to approach the Scriptures from a quite different viewpoint from that of most churchgoers. He knows, as quite probably his parents who are supposed to favour compulsory religious instruction do not, that the Bible is *not* true historically, geographically, ethnically, or, very largely, ethically. If, from the beginning of his biblical studies, the schoolboy has to be taught to treat his texts critically and to appreciate their deficiencies in so many respects, then he must be expected to use the same critical faculties on the religious assumptions concerning its moral authority. The earnest Scripture teacher is only too painfully aware of the difficulty in persuading twentieth-century youth, untrained in the niceties of theological hair-splitting, to appreciate the moral integrity of a god who demands the complete extermination of his Chosen People's enemies, and brings dire punishment upon any of his worshippers who dare to spare the lives of alien women and children. There is no less difficulty in explaining the motives of the same god who, in pursuit of some abstruse cosmic plan, leads a singularly gullible young rabbi to run foul of the Roman authorities and get himself executed, only to leave him hanging in agony on a cross in the bitterness of failure and loneliness. All this, the teacher has to persuade his restive class, is a manifestation of this god's love towards mankind; the more obvious deficiencies that mar the divine portrait in the Bible stem not from God's character but from man's inabilities to appreciate its finer points. If God seems to the reader cruel, even callous, it is because pain and suffering is at the heart of the universe, and through them man reaches spiritual perfection. In any case, God had not really abandoned Jesus on the cross: thirty-six hours later he arose from the grave and walked about talking to people, alive and well. Some six weeks later he disappeared into thin air, which is why no one ever found his mortal remains, however hard his rascally compatriots tried. And if the teacher's pupils show even less readiness to believe the story, he points to the existence of the Church and the New Testament to prove the point, since if Jesus had not survived, nobody would ever have heard the tale.

Quite apart from the difficulties of persuading a modern youth to believe this unlikely narrative and to assent to the dubious logic of the last proposition, the teacher has been obliged to plunge into dogmatic theology to explain the validity of the Bible as a moral authority. Thus the idea, currently held in educational circles, that the Bible can be taught to schoolchildren without taking a theological position is patently false. Of course, the various myths and legends of the Bible can be taught, and as pieces of ancient literature some are very fine, although not all are very edifying. But this presumably is not what our religious educationalists really want; they believe that teaching the Scriptures brings a child in touch with theological, particularly Christian, ideas and that these must necessarily urge them towards higher moral standards.

Our recent researches have shown that the Gospel story is not only quite unhistorical but was never intended to be more than a 'cover' for the activities and secret formulae of a sect despised by the Romans as drug-takers and trouble-makers. In so far as the much-vaunted moral teachings of the New Testament are valid homiletics, they were directed towards the members of a closely knit esoteric organization and not to the world at large. In any case, even those teachings at all comprehensible, and not on their face reading amoral or even immoral, lack sufficient context to be anything more than generalized expressions of reasonable behaviour. They need further elaboration and pointed application to specific cases to be really useful.

When we speak of the high moral ideals inculcated by the New Testament we are really talking of perhaps a dozen sayings which, over two millennia, have been interpreted and re-interpreted by the Church for the edification of the faithful. At their best, and brought down to practical teaching by wise counsellors, they have indeed served as valuable guides to humane conduct in man's affairs. But more often than not, it is the interpretation of the words that have served such a beneficial purpose, rather than the sayings themselves. As the Catholic Church has always maintained, it is the Church which is the source of understanding of the Scriptures; without her divine guidance the interpretation of the Bible is a hazardous task and not to be entrusted to the layman. That is why children of Catholic parents cannot join with their non-Catholic friends in the State's compulsory classes in religious education. Whatever 'heresies' the teacher may impart to others, the children of the true Church can receive their religious instruction only from one empowered by the Catholic authorities to impart it. Thus, from the beginning of their schooldays, a rift is driven between children of Catholic and non-Catholic upbringing which the Church ensures is continued throughout life. Thus, far from bringing children together and helping them to live with one another in mutual tolerance and understanding, the State, by enforcing religious teaching in the schools, divides children and helps sow the seeds of bigotry.

Much as we may deplore the attitude of separatism pursued by the Catholic Church, we have at least to acknowledge her logical consistency in the matter. She has not fallen into the sentimental fallacy of believing that by putting a Bible into the hands of a person you can teach him to be a good Christian. It is the interpretation of the writings that is important, and this is not a mere academic exercise but primarily a religious exposition. In other words, the Church rightly says that if you are going to teach the Scriptures with a view to imparting moral teaching, you must do it within the context of theological exposition. There is no such thing as secular religious instruction, except in purely comparative terms.

Of recent years, the educational authorities have shifted their position somewhat regarding religious instruction in schools. Faced with the increasing resistance on the part of non-church-going parents to having their children indoctrinated with any one denominational form of Christianity, and the difficulty of finding believing Christian schoolteachers to undertake the task with any competence, there is a tendency now to stress the importance of teaching comparative religion. Here, it seems, we are on safer ground. Surely not even the most bigoted Baptist parents would object to a Methodist teacher teaching Hinduism to their child. Again, it should not be too difficult to find agnostic or even atheist teachers to study the various world religions sufficiently to make their teaching interesting to the young Christians and pagans in the classroom. The only difficulty comes in those classes containing the children of Pakistani or Hindu immigrants who might well object to the presentation of their faith by non-believers. They then feel obliged to withdraw their children from those classes, and the much-sought integration of the white and coloured children is immediately set back a notch or two.

However, for the remaining western children, intrigued by the religious customs and beliefs of the strange people across the seas, the boring old class in religious instruction takes on new interest, and the headmaster breathes again. The teacher, too, is stimulated to new efforts and projects are devised to make first-hand acquaintance with living examples of non-christian religious practices. What, one might ask, could be better for understanding and mutual tolerance? But hold a while; is this the intended purpose of the compulsory class in religious instruction? If the children are to be taught as much about Buddha as Christ, Siva as Moses, Muhammad as Amos, what becomes of the inculcation of Christian morals for which we are told our parents long? And if these classes in comparative religion are on this purely academic basis, as objective studies of how other people worship, why should it be treated in any other way than normal school teaching by demanding a compulsory syllabus?

It may be fashionable to be broadminded about other religions, and as a means of persuading non-churchgoing parents to agree to religious instruction classes for their children in secular schools, comparative religion syllabuses are wonderfully attractive. But the people who devise these courses for the Ministry of Education and who staff our university theological faculties are mainly convinced Christians whose prime object is to evangelize the Faith. They are not in business to proclaim the authority of Buddha, Siva, or Muhammad, and the excellence of their religious and moral teachings. 'We preach Christ crucified' is the banner of their profession, and the religion of the Christ is not *primus inter pares;* it is unique. In His Son God revealed Himself to the world. There can be no more perfect revelation of the nature of the one deity. All other faiths are mere shadows, only here and there reflecting the majesty of God. In Christ, God stands revealed; in His sacrifice on the Cross, God made a once-for-all redemptive act for mankind. There cannot be two Christs, or three, or four . . . there cannot be more than one Atonement. Other religions may have inspired moral teachings worthy of the highest esteem, and may have produced from their followers great saints among men, like the Hindu Gandhi. Some of their sayings, indeed, make more sense than a few of those attributed to Jesus, but Christianity's moral centre lies not in homiletics but in the Cross on Calvary.

When the churches lend their vocal support for compulsory religious instruction in schools, and their leaders and academics write to the newspapers urging that all children should be 'exposed' to Christian teaching from the age of five onwards, they are not asking for them to be given a sampling of all the world religions and left to make up their own minds. Some of the teenagers might find more to interest them in the eroticism of the Kama Sutra than the Psalms, or even wonder if the humility and self-effacement of Gandhi had more to commend it than the public 'image' of some of the Church's more publicity-conscious clergy. Honesty would compel the clerical supporters of a wider religious syllabus in the schools to admit that their aim is to have 'contrastive' rather than comparative religion taught. Christianity would shine forth as a far, far better thing than any other faith, and the moral deficiencies of the rest would be clearly manifest even to the dimmest pupil.

Given equal time and emphasis in this comparative 'exposure' we might reasonably doubt that this assumption is valid. In practice, the personal preference of the teacher is almost certain to weigh the scales, so that the instruction easily becomes inculcation of the claims of one Faith over the others. If the object of the whole exercise is to teach children to be good, it is difficult to see how it can be presented otherwise. It is no use teaching other people's moral standards as of equal worth with your own, if you want your listeners to follow you.

At the root of this whole question of religious education lies this extraordinary but widespread fallacy that religion and morals are synonymous. One would have thought that the most cursory survey of the attitudes and actions of avowedly religious people around the world would have taught otherwise. Many of the world's religions, particularly those which emphasize the mystical communion between god and worshipper, are quite amoral. The mystic is not concerned with the world or his fellow man. Other religions, like Catholicism and Islam, are heavily concerned with political movements, and have often justified actions which the rest of us would consider highly immoral, subjugating the rights of the individual to an overriding political cause. Religion is, as we have seen, a highly divisive emotion, and if morality means living together in harmony, to abandon oneself to an irrational belief and set of prejudices can be no inducement to finding common humanitarian ground with strangers.

Too often this cry for religious teaching in schools is nothing more than a tacit admission by parents of their own failure in equipping their children with moral preparedness for life. They hope that by insisting on their offspring listening to an exposition of the Scriptures in the classroom once a week and each day singing a hymn in assembly, they can make up for the inadequacy of their home training. Yet it is from the same quarter that the fiercest opposition comes from proposals to teach sex relationships in schools. They would rather their daughter prepared for an evening out with her boyfriend with a hymn and a profound knowledge of the history of the kings of Israel, than an appreciation of the workings of her own and her companion's mind and body. Even the Ten Commandments are not really much help in helping a girl to decide how far she can let the boy go on a park bench.

By all means, let us have some form of moral instruction taught in our schools as part of the regular syllabus of education. Enlightened teachers, faced with the burden of making the compulsory religious instruction classes meaningful to their unbelieving pupils, have often adapted those periods to such useful purposes. The problem here is that the clerical advisers to the Ministry of Education have required a syllabus that leads to State examinations based primarily upon biblical studies, the history of the Jews, and the purport of Judaism and Christianity. So however usefully a teacher might employ the relevant periods of instruction for teaching the children about how a community is formed, derives its mores, imposes its own sanctions, and so on, his more advanced students are obliged to concentrate on biblical mythology and the more 'respectable' aspects of ancient Near Eastern religion for the benefit of some ecclesiastical examination panel.

It is far more important to teach our children the fundamentals of how communities and nations may live together in peace, and how we have to develop a world-wide system of government for the common good which will yet allow room for ethnic and cultural individuality. These ideas in their simplest form can be taught to the youngest schoolchild, since the family is a microcosm of the community, and the classroom is the first step towards the enlargement of the child's horizons to a global view of life. They can also be taught without distinction to Catholic and Protestant, Jew and Muslim, Sikh and Hindu, without dividing the classroom and setting barriers between children and their playmates, as the clerics would have us do.

The fact is that learning to live together is so important and its problems so immediate that we cannot afford to waste time and effort seeking means of teaching our children the irrelevancies of religious cults and creeds. Such instruction as part of a course at advanced levels on anthropology would be interesting and profitable, but it has little or no part in the teaching of ethics and civics, which should be essentially practical in conception and purpose.

Once we can divorce morality from religion in our minds, and separate social wrongdoing from theological sin, we can clear the ground and set out clearly the bases on which we judge good and evil. Children are perfectly able to discern between them; it does not need a school visitor wearing his collar back to front and talking about God and heaven and gentle Jesus for a child to know that if he hammers Jake in the playground he is going to be hammered back and may come off worse. If he steals Sue's sweets, she'll tell teacher and he will be hauled before the whole class and made to feel small and silly. He soon learns that within his small community bullying does not pay or earn lasting respect, but that kindness and gentleness to the underdog win him gratitude and the praise of those whom he most loves. This kind of moral philosophy may not be deep or involved, but it is at least easily comprehensible and seen to be effective. If a child does wrong, the effects are soon noticeable either on himself or other people. His actions are not determined by their influence for good or ill on an Old Gentleman in the sky. The child's moral perspective is focused on his family and school, not on heaven and hell. In later years he must shift it to larger horizons, to the world at large and the continuing life of the community. But it is in his formative years, through trial and error, and through the precept and example of those he most respects, that the groundwork of adult morality is laid.

The easiest and the worst way of teaching ethics is with a big stick. Whether brandished physically by the parent or teacher, or metaphorically with threats of hell and a divine bogyman, this kind of moral enforcement pays ever-decreasing dividends. Its cost in terms of the young child's personality, and particularly in the sapping of his self-confidence, is such that mercifully it is falling out of favour among more enlightened parents and teachers. Certain branches of the Church, particularly Catholicism, still manage to maintain a discipline of fear, but this too must eventually decline as the authority of the priest diminishes. To be scared of the watchful eye of God demands first a belief in a deity and then a firm conviction that power for judgement resides in the Church's hierarchy. When these assumptions wear thin and gradually vanish altogether, other more rational persuasions to self-control and altruism become necessary. This is why an early, non-religious moral training is so important. Living harmoniously with our neighbours is far too vital a feature of life to be dependent upon the vagaries of theological speculation.

Nowadays we profess ourselves deeply concerned with the slackening of self-discipline in our 'permissive' society. Not a little of the call for religious teaching in schools stems from the fear of parents that, once freed from parental care, their young will take to the streets and drug themselves to death or be infected almost immediately with venereal disease. Certainly tragic examples of this kind of folly are in the news every day, and sometimes the tragedy strikes nearer home among people we know, and even in our own families. There is no doubt at all that young people are more independent than they have ever been. More go away from home to universities, and more can afford to live in lodgings or share flats in other towns and cities where jobs are plentiful and well paid. They have to learn to stand on their own feet quicker than used to be the case, and new-found freedom is a heady drug. It is to be expected that many will fall and make mistakes. The weak will certainly go to the wall, and society must pay the price in broken hearts and homes, and in the stretching of its resources to provide remedial centres for the repair of bruised bodies and minds. But what is the alternative? Is it to tie our children more firmly to their mother's apron strings, to shelter them from the perils of the world, to curb their restiveness with the strap or by cutting off their pocket money?

Those days are past. We must see to it that our young are equipped for the world beyond our front doors with an adequate understanding of what real life is all about. That can hardly be done by spending valuable classroom time on discussing the fortunes of a Semitic tribe who seemed to spend most of their time slaughtering their neighbours when they were not killing each other. By dint of much imagination and determined exegesis it might be possible to discover in the history of the ancient Jews valuable lessons on how to treat landladies, bosses, sharers of communal bathrooms, work-mates, and a girl friend who has trusted you not to bring her to harm. But a few well-directed words and above all demonstration within the home of care for other people's feelings will serve the fledgling far better when he spreads his wings for the first time.

We are told that the prime reason for the young person becoming addicted to drugs is a sense of inadequacy. Looking at the kind of world into which our youth are precipitated from their schools and colleges, this is hardly surprising. Never before have their minds been subjected to so much battering by the advertising media to buy, buy, buy. . . . The successful men and women have to eat this, smoke that, dress in this, drive in that. Everything they see on the television screens and in the glossy magazines contrasts with what they have and are. If these creatures of the advertisers' chimera are the successful ones then they, the public, are unsuccessful, inadequate. However much they try, whatever they do, eat, wear or drive, they will never match this ideal.

Since young people are subjected to intense advertising from the moment they can understand children's programmes on sponsored television, the debunking process cannot begin too soon. It is a sad fact of modern life that we need to teach our children to disbelieve what they see and hear almost as soon as we inculcate honesty and obedience. We have to instruct them in cynicism, to criticize and laugh at the unreal absurdities of the professional persuader. They must know from the age of four of five about the double standards of truth that adults purvey: that the sweets and comic papers and toys displayed on the television screen for their adulation are not necessarily the 'best', 'brightest', or 'most longed-for' of their kind. Grownups are paid to say this by others who want to be rich. We may well ask ourselves what sort of society we have created that allows children to be sucked into the screaming, hideous vortex of the ad-mass, to have their ideas and standards manipulated by an industry whose sole purpose is to control people's minds and urge them into courses of action their reason would otherwise resist. But having nourished this fearful abortion in our midst, we have now to teach our young to withstand its blandishments. They have to learn to think for themselves and to call the advertiser a liar and a cheat. It has somehow to be brought home to them that real happiness is not to be attained, or its depth measured, in terms of the sweetest candies, the glossiest comic papers, or the most coveted toys, nor in later life even in the possession of mink and fast cars, but in the right relationships they achieve with their fellows.

How, we may ask of our protagonists for religious instruction, are our children going to be trained in critical thinking by persuading them emotionally to accept an irrational Faith? Does overriding the conclusions of their reasoned judgements by dogmatic theological assertions about God and a divine purpose really help to form their critical faculties? Constant repetition, accompanied by pious exegesis, has often dulled our appreciation of the absurdities and cruelties of many of the biblical narratives and teachings. Children see with a clearer eye, as religious teachers in schools find to their constant embarrassment. They have a disconcerting way of siding with the religious outcast against the righteous prig, and of asking pertinent questions about the fair play exemplified by some of Jehovah's more arbitrary judgements. When the Bible tells them that the crafty Jacob tricking his brother Esau out of his rights, or deceiving his father-in-law Laban and stealing his flocks, or doing a ten per cent deal with his god in return for special favours, is demonstrating goodness worthy of a patriarch of Israel, the child may be excused for wondering why his own ideas of honesty should be so much at variance with those of this hero of the Bible. His teacher's explanation of the limited appreciation by the Scriptural writers of God's justice must surely leave the youthful enquirer with a set of double standards hardly less confusing than the discrepancies between truth and fiction he has been taught to recognize in the television commercials.

If we decide to relieve the schools of this burden of compulsory religious instruction and assemblies, and ask that the time so saved be used for teaching the fundamentals of communal living and the resistance to disseminated false values, how shall we train staff to specialize in this subject? For training there ought to be. There will be a tendency for hard-pressed education authorities to close down the religious departments of their teachers' training colleges and let moral education in the schools go by default to any teacher the headmaster can coerce or simply draft into the job, just as religious teaching has been treated in the past. Certainly, once ethics have been divorced from religion in education, the need for specialized college training in biblical studies will cease. Such advanced courses in comparative religion for sixth-form and college work can be quite adequately provided by the universities and their extra-mural departments.

But the teaching of moral philosophy and civics is far too

important to be left to the untrained but good-hearted soul with a period or two free each week. It is a serious subject and needs to be taught at least as professionally as Bible studies and with much more practical application. Training courses should be devised with the aid of our university philosophy and social administration departments to cater for every level of school instruction, and with as little interference from university theological faculties as possible.

Full time training in the colleges in these and related subjects would provide not only a body of teachers able to introduce our young people to a disciplined study of communal living, but a nucleus of adults trained for social service. With the demise of the Church, these are the people who will eventually replace the parish priest. Having no denominational or class loyalties they will be far better placed than the clerics to perform their function of social welfare, and with no less regard for the personalities and idiosyncrasies of their protégés. As life becomes more and more organized, and the rights of the individual come under increasing pressure before the need for efficient administration of the community, so the necessity will grow for counsellors to whom ordinary folk can turn for help, advice and, above all, comfort. This will be a quite different service from that rendered by the nine-to-five official who mans the information desks in our town halls. Theirs will be a dedicated work of self-involvement in the lives and cares of their fellows of the kind demonstrated by the best parish vicar. Happily for the future of mankind, there will always appear such people who can subordinate their own wellbeing to the assistance of those less fortunate in talents or material possessions. Until now many of them have found the outlet for their charity (in the proper sense of that word) through the ministrations of the Church, whilst not necessarily assenting to her doctrines or discipline. Indeed often they have found her sectarianism a hindrance to their efforts in helping the unbelieving member of the community. Furthermore, their work has usually been on a voluntary and unpaid basis, which has limited the numbers of people who can spend of their time and money to serve the community.

The training colleges might well hold courses in moral and social welfare, not only for teachers but simultaneously, or in the vacations, for full-time counsellors who will be paid certainly no less than their academic colleagues by the local authorities. The strange attitude that still prevails in our country that a full-time professional social worker is less humanely activated than her voluntary, untrained counterpart must give way before a realistic appreciation of the need for proper training in the field of human relations. An immense amount of damage can be done by kind, well-meaning people who involve themselves in the emotional affairs of others without adequate psychological knowledge nor the humility to refer cases beyond their competence to a professional consultant. Some clerics are particularly prone to this failing, aggravated in their case by their conviction that prayer and self-examination are necessary channels of divine grace and healing. This kind of introspective treatment administered to certain types of psychological disorder can well be disastrous.

Of course, there will always be room for the voluntary, unpaid welfare worker. The time, energy and money that is presently directed towards running bazaars, sponsored walks and tea-parties for the upkeep of dilapidated church buildings, organ funds and so on, could well be channelled into serving the community more usefully. But those with good intent and time on their hands should be encouraged to undergo a course of training in moral and social welfare work, so that their endeavours may be used for the benefit of their fellows as efficiently as possible. Belonging to this or that religious order, or owning an under-employed car, are not really sufficient qualifications for taking upon oneself responsibility for advising the mentally or emotionally troubled.

To summarize, then: the strange notion that 'exposing' a school child to the Bible and Christianity at an early age sets him automatically on the path to morality has nothing to support it. The Old Testament, never a very satisfactory handbook of ancient history, has even less relevance as a source of moral teaching for the twentieth century. In any case, as Catholicism has long recognized, the Bible cannot be so used outside the ministrations of the Church; there is no such thing as secularly taught biblical morality. Thus the whole conception of religious instruction in State schools without sectarian indoctrination is false, and imposes an impossible task on non-believing teachers unwilling to compromise with truth and their own integrity.

Much of the pressure for compulsory religious education in state schools derives from a popular confusion between religion and morality. Parents, often themselves without any religious affiliation and swayed by clerical propaganda, have been persuaded into pressing for such instruction in the vain hope that their children will thereby be led to the good life. Whilst many schools have attempted to translate this ill-advised directive into moral instruction and teaching of civics, the syllabus laid down for their pupils who wish to pursue their studies in this field relates specifically to biblical knowledge. Although wider studies of religion generally are now becoming more fashionable, they belong properly to advanced courses in the field of anthropology. In any case, they have little or no bearing on the teaching of moral philosophy.

The decline in religious belief and the recognition of the distinction between religion and ethics make any continuance of this policy of compulsory religious instruction purposeless. However, the need for moral training in its widest sense is even more pressing. Teaching a child to be good is primarily the function of parenthood within the home environment; nevertheless academic instruction on the nature of the community and the individual's part in it would be a valuable part of school teaching. In that case, training of teachers for this work needs to be carefully devised and carried out, using the facilities at present allotted to Bible studies. Such courses would also provide a means for building up a reserve of trained counsellors to replace the clerical father-confessors to whom persons in need of comfort and advice have turned in the past. Without the barriers of sectarian religious divisiveness, we need not doubt that the fount of human charity, effectively channelled where the need is greatest, will adequately compensate for those humanitarian functions of the Church which must now inevitably decline.

CHAPTER ELEVEN

Christenings, Weddings and Funerals

MOST people in this supposedly 'Christian' country have only a threefold acquaintance with the Church: at baptism, marriage and death. The ceremonies of the christening, wedding and the funeral may be devoid of any deeply religious significance for our pagan community, but they are nevertheless part of the traditional pattern of folk behaviour and have roots deep in the social consciousness. The celebration of a birth and reception of the infant into the community, the giving of a name by which the baby becomes a recognizable member of a society, is marked by tribal ceremonies the world over. Similarly, plighting one's troth to the woman of one's choice before the community, and taking a joint farewell of a respected elder at death, are important features of any communal life. Certainly the shutting of churches is not likely to diminish these occasions in their importance, although their forms and symbolism may be expected to change. Indeed, it would do no great harm if some aspects of the ceremonies were re-examined for their real meaning and validity, and a great deal of the over-sentimentality and mock piety associated with them were to disappear.

At its christening a child is received into the community of Christians. The parents pledge to bring their child up in a specifically religious fashion, teaching it Christian doctrine and ensuring its continuance in the Faith. How many of the parents proudly displaying their offspring before their friends at the altar have the slightest intention of fulfilling their vows made on that occasion, or indeed have even bothered to take note of what they are promising, must be very few to judge from their later attendances at worship. In the popular mind the christening ceremony is a means of giving the child a name, receiving on its behalf a number of gifts, most of them quite useless, and basking in the shared joy of their relations and friends. It is, quite properly, a supremely happy and proud occasion, and for most the impropriety of making false declarations of intent before the deity never obtrudes to mar the festive occasion.

If most parsons are prepared to join in the fun, fully aware of the insincerity of the chief participants' religious affirmations but hoping that something of their import might stick and be later recalled, other clerics have rebelled against what they have not unfairly regarded as a farce and a mockery of God and His Church. Every so often the newspapers carry stories of enraged pagan parents being refused this office of the Church for their offspring on the grounds that they clearly had no intention of carrying out their vows. Unfortunately, the Church of England is in a difficult position in this respect, being the established church of the country. Many laymen appear to think of the Church as their property, a kind of nationalized God-service. If Anglican clergy are too forcible in pointing out the obvious fallacy of this belief, they run the danger of raising the perennial question of disestablishment and the public airing of the ever-growing disquiet within the Church about the incongruity of its position in a largely pagan society, when even its prayerbook has to be approved by the House of Commons.

Of course, the sincere clerics who disapprove of their churches being used for ceremonial purposes only, by people who have no regard for the religion the buildings are supposed to represent, are perfectly right. They should turn applicants for the Church's offices away from the doors if they are not willing to obey the rules. The Church is not a nationalized industry, put there and maintained by the State for its convenience. In making this position plain once and for all, the Anglicans should then go on and face, fairly and squarely without any more hedging, this question of disestablishment. If the Church is going to remain in business at all, it can only be as a purveyor of religion, not as a second-rate 'Oxfam', soup-kitchen or even a State 'Palace of Culture' on the Soviet pattern. It may hurt the pride of the corps of empurpled bishops to be removed from their bench in the House of Lords, or from their ability to decree whom members of the Royal Family may and may not marry, but at least the Church of England could call its soul its own and decide thereafter whom it allows through its doors and admits to its sacred offices. Until then, its priests must be prepared to endure the tragi-comedy of pagan 'christenings', weddings and funerals in the name of its god.

Of more importance for the rest of us is to decide what these ceremonies represent to us, what is worth keeping and what can be dispensed with in a modern godless society. There seems no reason why some formal presentation of a newly born infant by its parents to the community should not be devised, involving a conscientious dedication of themselves to serving their fellows and a promise to bring up the child with an awareness of his responsibilities to the community. Such avowals could at least be made more honestly by the unbeliever than his promises to bring up the child 'in the faith of the Lord Jesus Christ'. Even if the lofty arches and smell of stale incense smoke has to be surrendered to the twentieth-century architecture of a well-lit and aired community centre, the surroundings do at least reflect the time and purpose of the ceremony, and the kind of matter-of-fact world in which the child is to be reared. And the poor infant would be spared the indignity of having a stubby ecclesiastical finger describing mystic symbols over its face with cold water.

Much the same objections as can be raised on pagan 'christenings' relate to pagan weddings in church. In these cases, however, the clouding of motives by over-sentimentalism, and the obscuring of real purpose by the orange blossom and floating veils of white tulle, is a very much more serious matter and a cause for concern. The divorce rate in this country has never been so high, and the toll these failures must take on the lives of the children of such ill-starred marriages is incalculable. How many broken pledges of lifetime fidelity and love were made at the altar of a god to whom neither party owed any allegiance? The only Scriptures or doctrinal tracts many such couples are likely to have read would have been a sixpenny pamphlet of wedding etiquette and a somewhat more expensive tome on how to find the most suitable position for enjoyable copulation. Many earnest parsons, approached by strangers wanting to marry in his church, will try to ensure that before the great day he has had a chance to talk to them about their religious responsibilities. But since in most cases their common ground of discussion will be negligible, there is little chance of the priest's being able to indoctrinate them into the nature and purpose of the Church, let alone convert them to the Faith, in a couple of thirty-minute sessions. The girl's mind is more likely to be filled with thoughts of her dress, bridesmaids, trousseau and resisting mother's choice of Uncle Herbert as speech-maker on behalf of the family; the man's on how many pub-crawls are left to him in his sadly waning period of liberty. The result is that when the happy couple sign the register in blissful relief that the best man had not lost the ring, and neither had fluffed their responses, they are very little wiser about the nature of the religious ceremony they have just undergone, nor the extraordinary promises they have made to one another. Furthermore, by their agreeing to be married under the auspices of the Church, they have assented to the proposition that 'those whom God has joined together let no man put asunder'; in other words, divorce under any man-made law is out of the question. The Catholic Church is still adamant on this point; the Anglicans prevaricate; but the wording of the marriage service to which the young pagans have submitted is clear.

Now this is not going to stop our young bright-eyed newly-weds rushing off to lawyers a couple of years later demanding a divorce. They may well have good reasons for doing so, not least of them being the fact that they should not have married in the first place. They had nothing in common but a mania for some pop group, an ability to perform the same gyrations and body-squirming on a dance floor, and nowadays more often than not, a capability of achieving simultaneous orgasms in bed. The real tragedy of these situations is, of course, the child they managed to bring into the world in that time. From the morning the growing foetus gave the mother nausea, the baby became a nuisance and heralded the eventual dissolution of the marriage.

Would the marriage have ever taken place, we may wonder, if the girl had thought beyond the glamour of a 'white wedding', of which a solemnization in the parish church is such a necessary part in the popular imagination? For years she has feasted her mind and imagination on the pictures presented to her in the television advertisements. The radiant bride, dressed of course by Hartnell, appears before the church door and laughingly (teeth by Colgate) tosses her bouquet to envious girl friends. In the background stands a handsome, smiling, fully robed vicar, and beside her the immaculately dressed (Moss Bros) groom and father and stunningly coutured mother (slimmed for the occasion by Spirella). A Rolls-Royce purrs to the old lichgate, and whisks the happy couple off to the Riviera for their fabulous honeymoon (by Cook's). The picture fades to a dream-kitchen in Sevenoaks, washed clean by invisible hands wielding waterless mops soaked in a wonder detergent. An oh-so-sweet little girl trips in to enquire of her perfectly manicured mother how she has kept her oh-so-smooth hands free from signs of manual toil . . . and so on.

Would not this dream world have been shattered into some semblance of reality had the hopeful pair been refused one ingredient of the white wedding by a vicar who refused to marry a couple who had no serious or permanent church affiliations? Or if he had expressed himself willing to perform the ceremony only after an adequate course of religious and doctrinal instruction, at least as thorough as that imposed on young people at confirmation? Or if it had been sternly laid down that on no account were such pagan trappings as orange blossom, silver horseshoes and confetti to be brought into the church?

Suppose, then, having been deterred from the television dream to some extent by an uncooperative vicar, the pair were required by law to appear before a marriage counsellor whose task it was to instruct them both in the legal aspects of the marriage contract, and at the same time to probe kindly but firmly into their real intentions towards one another and any children of the union. Suppose, perhaps for the first time, the young man were thus suddenly made aware that marriage carried considerable financial responsibilities, and that having plighted his troth to the girl beside him he would be liable for all time to support her and their children whether he had tired of the union or not. Would he not take another calculating look at the girl and be inclined to think beyond the delights of the honeymoon and the car their joint income would buy and run, to the burden of wife and children his own wage would one day have to bear?

How much more ethical, not to say economical in view of ever-rising bill of supplementary benefits paid to deserted wives and unwanted offspring, it would be for the State to insist on such prior consultation and instruction before marriage rather than to allow young couples to be dazzled by specious advertising into dashing off to church at the first stir of the sex hormones.

And how much more effective such an interview might be if the bride-to-be were not blinded by white tulle and deafened to the voice of reason by the pealing of church bells.

One might wonder at the Church allowing its sacred offices to be used for decorative purposes by people with no religious affiliations or real interest, but we cannot blame her ministers for the State's failure to make sure that her young people understand the legal implications of the grave step they contemplate. These are not the Church's concern. Her first duty is to the religious aspects of the ceremony which is for the Church a sacred office and sacrament, not a legal undertaking. There is much to be said for the Continental system of observing the religious rites only after the civic formalities have been carried out at the town hall. At least the parties are made aware that they are entering primarily into a civil contract.

More and more couples are acknowledging the impropriety of undergoing religious rites in which they have no belief or real interest, and marrying at registry offices. Mothers brought up in the old tradition may secretly wonder if their daughters are not thereafter living in sin, but fathers at least appreciate not having to pay the parson, choir boys, bell-ringers and other beneficiaries of the 'white-wedding syndrome'. With the decline of the Church's influence and the decrease in places of worship available, this trend to a civic function will certainly gather momentum. We may hope that the resultant unfashionableness of white church weddings will take away some of the false glamour of the marriage ceremony and its superficial attractiveness to the television-reared girl. Nevertheless, the legal requirement of signing a register should not be the only recognition of this important event in the lives of two young people.

Marriage should be a supremely happy occasion, and one to be shared by the community to which the couple belong, as well as by relatives and intimate acquaintances. The event has much in common in this respect with the 'naming ceremony' for young babies, since the community has in both cases a responsibility to declare towards its members and their welfare. As our societies become ever more closely integrated, the assumption by the group of responsibilities for its weaker members becomes increasingly necessary. As a baby may be thrown upon the mercies of the community through the default of its parents, or its incapability of surviving the pressures of normal life through some deformity or mental defect, so a marriage which breaks down almost inevitably makes claims upon the community's welfare facilities. It would be fitting therefore that a wedding celebration should include some gathering of well-wishers including representatives of the local legislature, in a semi-formal ceremony of congratulation. The atmosphere, less rigid and legalistic than the register office but more serious than the wedding breakfast convivialities to follow, would aim again at conveying to all concerned the involvement of the whole community in the marriage union of two of its members.

To an ever-increasing degree, the choice of partner in marriage affects the rest of society. Neglected wives and children and deformed babies need the help of the others, so it would seem only right that the marriage should be seen by the community to be setting off on the right lines. As well as ensuring that both parties are aware of their legal and moral responsibilities, there is a case for the State requiring that they undergo medical examinations before being granted their marriage licence. Whilst it might not be possible or desirable in a free society to forbid persons with serious physical or mental disabilities from marrying, at least they could be made aware of any special difficulties that might arise in conception or childbirth which would prepare them for necessary hospitalization or disappointment. We may hope that the results of present researches into genetic control will one day ensure that women never bear mongol or similarly malformed offspring, but to exercise such control it will be necessary to make the medical tests here suggested as a prerequisite to marriage.

Again, to insist on medical examinations of intending spouses would emphasize further the serious nature of the step they intend taking. One can see that it might in some cases involve some desperate soul-searching if a defect were brought to light in one of the partners of which the other was ignorant, or indeed which was unsuspected by the victim. Should a man, for example, carry on with his plans to marry a girl who would probably never bear a live or normal child? Should a woman commit herself to someone for life who has suffered from venereal disease and whose blood can never be considered absolutely clear of the virus? If it be argued that to involve a young couple in such grave considerations when they are enjoying the emotional flights of their romance is wanton cruelty, one must answer that these facts are better faced before the union than after, unless we are going to continue filling our divorce courts with psychologically bruised people and their hapless offspring.

The Church's main interest in the selection of partners in marriage has been to ensure that as far as possible 'mixed' marriages, that is between Catholics and non-Catholics, should be avoided. If a mixed marriage is enacted, the Church insists that its progeny should be educated in obedience to the Catholic Faith whatever the wishes of the other spouse. Thus, from the very moment of marriage, the Church manages to divide husband from wife in a way that is bound later on to be aggravated by squabbles over the children's upbringing, to say nothing of the conflicting views they will probably hold about birth-control. Again, to the outsider it seems extraordinary that rational human beings should allow their lives to be dictated in this way by a celibate clergy. We can but look forward to a lessening of this alienating influence in man's affairs, and to a time when men and women will choose each other for life mates solely on the grounds of their mutual love and willingness to share a lifetime's joys and responsibilities.

The last occasion on which the Church figures in our mortal existence is after death. For most of us this is an involuntary submission to the Church's offices, but for the Catholic believer the priest's ministrations at the moment of death as well as at the interment and thereafter are crucial to the soul's smooth path to heaven. Even an innocent babe, straight from the womb and as yet unbaptized, cannot pass beyond the intermediary stage of purgatory without the last rites being performed on its behalf. Non-christians can only wonder at the nature of this god who can make a child's life in the hereafter dependent upon its being doused with water and prayed over before death.

We have already discussed the idea of the hereafter and suggested that with the abandonment of religious belief our conception of a continuing life will tend to be restricted to this earthly scene. We live on in the lives of our children or in the community as a whole. The old nature philosophers saw a continuing cycle of life through birth and death and rebirth entirely within an earthly perspective, and if our sense of purpose demands a view stretching beyond the death of the individual, we should probably find our assurance in a similar practical philosophy.

But this is not the Christian view. When the parson stands by the graveside and commits the body to the ground or crematorium furnace, he speaks of God 'taking unto Himself the soul of our brother here departed', and of a 'certain hope of the resurrection to eternal life through our Lord and Saviour Jesus Christ.' He reads passages from the Bible which seem to promise a place for the believer in heaven: 'in my Father's House are many mansions. . . . I go to prepare a place for you'; 'we have a building from God, a house not made with hands, eternal, in the heavens', and so on. The Church took the myth of the dying and rising god, personified as a man Jesus, and proclaimed the story of his resurrection as historical proof that there is life after death and that the believer can look forward to his spiritual existence in another world. This aspect of the Church's teaching has seemed to many a blessed consolation in times of bereavement. Lover and beloved would meet again in the presence of the risen Lord.

Now that the origin of the Jesus legend has been laid bare, and the 'resurrected Lord' is seen to have no more historical reality than a mushroom, has the bereaved no consolation? Must death seem only to deny the value of living, wiping clean the slate as if the deceased had never lived and all life's achievements and high intent cancelled out as vanity? Surely the Christian believer has looked to a life beyond death not because the Church assured him that a man who had been dead for a day and half suddenly started breathing again, but because immortality made sense of life. He could not bring himself to believe that the bond of a lifetime could be so easily broken by the accident of death. He looked for a continuity of existence, a longer perspective than a single lifetime, which would make the effort of living worthwhile.

This is really the message of the old fertility philosophy: life continues in one's family and in the community to which the individual has offered his life's work. Once we have rid ourselves of the Church's insistence that life only has meaning if the individual's soul lives on, and have shaken off fears of divine retribution to pay off old scores marked up during life, we can look at death with a more rational and balanced understanding.

Of course it is the end of an individual's life span. Why not? To many people it seems quite extraordinary that one should want to live on in some ghostly spirit world for ever and ever. And not all of us want to think of our loved ones floating around in space waiting for us or, worse, watching us and all that is going on in the world they have left. The merits and achievements of each person live on in the life of the family and community, and surely we can be grateful for our heritage without having to think of our forefathers hanging around aloft spying on what use we make of it. It is also true that the failures and wrongdoing of people live on after their deaths. The world will go on suffering for a long time yet from the bestiality of Hitler and his supporters, and the selfishness of those who thought they could buy time for themselves at the cost of small nations. A bullying husband and father can leave scars on the sensibilities of his wife and children which long outlive his death. Does it really help those who are left to bear the burden to imagine Hitler and the boorish father roasting in hell? Does the thought of a righteous God consigning the sinner to perdition really give us comfort and waken within us a sense of gratitude for divine justice? It is more likely to breed a spirit of smug self-righteousness that blinds us to our own faults.

For most people these days the religious ministrations that attend funerals have become merely part of the accepted tradition, on a par with the sombre garb of the hearse driver and his assistants and the ham-and-salad tea in the parlour afterwards. For a stipulated fee, included in the overall cost of corpse committal, a parson in full regalia will attend at the grave or alongside the coffin in the crematorium and go through the usual motions and incantations suitable for the occasion. The honest unbeliever obliged to attend this sham ritual may feel his gorge rise, but remains quiet in case some more pious member of the family may be receiving real comfort from the service. For those who have never really thought much about the religious implications of the burial service and are content to follow the rites without intellectual involvement, it may appear to be a kind of insurance policy for eternity. It cannot do any harm, and if it does save old George from hell-fire, it is probably worth the extra five guineas that the parson receives for his extra-mural activity.

But is it all really necessary? When it is well known that no member of the family of the deceased has any religious affiliations or interest, cannot this sham ritual be dispensed with? There is enough hypocrisy in the whole sordid business of corpse disposal without continuing with meaningless rites for the sake of appearances. At the same time, where the dead person was the subject of deep affection and his loss must bring real pain to his loved ones, anything which rings untrue can only make the occasion of his passing more bitter.

It is happily becoming more common for pagan mourners to gather at the crematorium in silence before the remains of their erstwhile companion, or listen to a brief and sincere eulogy from a friend or relative, and then go home and be thankful for the benefits the life that has ended bestowed upon his family and the community. Then those who sincerely subscribe to a religious belief in the afterlife and the power of their prayers to smooth the soul's passage through purgatory, may repair to a proper place of worship for the committal rites. It is only by thus separating true religious observances from secularist gatherings that the interests of the Church can be safeguarded and funerals relieved of the trappings and make-believe of mock piety.

The time has come, then, for us to take stock of our real sentiments and hopes at the natural climaxes of life, birth, marriage and death. These should be times of joy and compassion when families and friends join in acknowledging important events in the lives of their companions. We are in danger of losing genuine sentiment and deep emotion in a tide of cynicism created by the false values purveyed by advertising men and their media. Nothing is sacred from their obnoxious smear of commercialism. Every day the only true values left in this world, like human love, maternal pride and filial affection, are raped and despoiled in the cause of selling trash to a moronic public. We have to resist this debasement of our dearest possessions, and the first necessity is to clear our minds of what is valuable and what is not. If to most of us the trappings and regalia of outworn creeds and rituals mean nothing, then let us banish them from those moments of real significance in our lives. Let our babies be presented to the community, our young people to each other in marriage, and the achievements of the dead to those who survive them in solemn thanksgiving, without marring the occasions with the insincerity of meaningless religious rituals.

CHAPTER TWELVE

The End of a Road

RELIGION is part of growing up. It expresses by prayer and ritual a sense of dependence upon some power greater than man. It is an acknowledgement of his inadequacy, a confession of weakness. Religion offers the oppressed a bolt-hole from the world. Amid a hostile environment, man turns his face to heaven for assurance that he is after all a son of God. No matter how contemptuously fate may treat him, he is of ultimate worth and his vindication by God is certain.

The strength of religious institutions stands in inverse proportion to man's self-confidence in his ability to control his environment. A religious scientist of the top rank is a rare phenomenon. The churches are filled today with the elderly, and of those most are women. The young, attracted at first by the high idealism of a social gospel, turn away before adulthood when their optimistic fervour is threatened by extinction through the prevailing atmosphere of spiritual abasement. The pall of sin hangs heavy over the religionist; try as he will he cannot attain the heights of mystic unity with his god. He translates this failure in emotional self-absorption into terms of psychological inadequacy, and despairingly throws himself into even greater dependence upon the offices of his church. The young have no part in this, and look elsewhere for the vehicle of their enthusiasm for life and confidence in mankind.

Contrary to the fears of many parents for whom religion and the Church have ceased to have real meaning, their lack of faith in God will not drive their children on the road to ruin. They will not inspire young people to moral conduct by pretending to beliefs they do not hold and paying lip-service to conventional sentiments they inwardly despise. Nor will they achieve their aim by painting the world as entirely perfidious and morally corrupt in the hope that, thus warned, their children will resist its temptations to easy pleasure. Even if their efforts do not have the opposite effect of driving their youth to sample the fruits of this forbidden garden, they may destroy the one precious quality of the young that can save them from submergence in the slime: a belief in the future.

If we take away the sparkle of high expectancy from a child's eye, we slam a door in his mind. He grows sullen and discontented with himself and others if the future looks devoid of excitement. If, with our well-meant efforts to deter our young people from wrong, we paint too gloomy a picture of the world and its problems, we rob them of the incentive to do well. We lower their perspective of life, so that the silhouettes of foreboding blot out the horizon.

There are, of course, vast problems before us, and new ones present themselves every day as technological advances outstrip our moral capabilities. Foremost among our concerns must be the equitable balancing of the world's riches, as already discussed. Failure to do this on national and international levels must spell disaster for the whole of mankind. But problems like these are not to be solved by creeping into churches and praying to God to take pity on our insufficiencies. In the case of righting the balance of world resources and opportunities, the remedy lies in our own hands. We need only the foresight and moral courage to put it into effect. Other problems that we have discussed have no immediately discernible solution, particularly those which relate to the rights of the individual in a closely integrated society, and the giving and taking of life. There are no overriding principles that we can read from a book or learn from the lips of a Pope or Archbishop and then apply blindly to every case. If, as we have said, we are going to 'play God' we have to learn the rules for ourselves and hope that we make a better job of controlling our bodies and environment for the benefit of all than the deity of any religion so far has managed to achieve.

The first need is for self-confidence. It is just here that religion fails our need, for the primary principle of faith in God is an utter trust in His omniscience and omnipotence. There are times in every life when we long most of all for such a faith. Everything we touch goes wrong, our best endeavours turn sour on us, we lose the confidence of those who respected our judgements, we miss our way. At such times, to be able to turn into a church and submit our tortured minds to the balm of a confessional, or the soothing assurance of an age-old ritual and long-familiar texts and hymns, is to find a haven of peace from the storm. The fight for the moment is over; God in His wisdom has ordained the tempest in our lives, but has now brought us back into port calm in the certainty that come what may He guards us and will eventually bring us to Himself. He knows the situation and the answers; we don't. We fight against the inevitable and destroy our own peace of mind. Relax, says the religious pacifier, you are impotent before God; let Him carry you over the bad patches.

This is fine, but the problems are still there when we leave the church's haven. The best that our temporary sojourn in the arms of the Lord has achieved is a breathing space and a period of quiet to collect our thoughts for the next round. But we still have to grapple with life ourselves, and merely to drift along airily consigning our worries to God and hoping He or someone else will take them from us, solves nothing and will usually mean that others suffers eventually from our indecision.

We are continually told that people need religion. This may be true of some, although it is remarkably seldom that the person affirming this general principle will acknowledge a similar dependence on his own part. It is emphatically not true of all, and it is to those who refuse to sink wearily back into the arms of an all-knowing God when faced with seemingly insurmountable problems that mankind must look for moral progress. We do not all need religion: we do need self-confidence, and the two are incompatible. Above all our young people need to learn to stand on their own feet, and to subject them to a posture of self-humiliation before a god or priest from an early age with some vague idea of knocking the cockiness out of them and making them 'good' is the first step towards driving them to delinquency. Fostering in the minds of the young a feeling of inadequacy from the start is the best way parents and teachers can provide work for future generations of welfare workers and psychoanalysts, to say nothing of a soft market for the advertising industry. Unless such children can soon throw off the shackles that have been placed around their minds and personalities and stand erect, they will never be able to face alone the challenge of life's problems, or sift for themselves the good from the bad.

For some years now the Church has been fast losing ground. The Protestant confessions were the first to slide, since their authority depended too much on a free consensus of opinion to withstand the impact of nineteenth-century rationalism. If it takes fifty or even a hundred years for the clergy to come round to accepting scientific propositions that their laity had agreed to from the start, they can hardly claim to be leaders of thought. A Church which is so blinded by its traditions and dogma that it cannot bring itself to accept well-founded scientific propositions about the origin of the world and mankind, cannot be expected to offer reasonable solutions to day-to-day problems raised by a technological society.

The Catholic Church could rest for much longer on its

internal discipline. Its people were not supposed to assent intellectually to either its dogma or its moral teaching. On that basis, the findings of Charles Darwin and his colleagues could have no possible impact upon the Church's teaching. She gained her knowledge not from watching monkeys but by direct revelation from God; truth is the prerogative of the Church alone, and that is that. Now even that authority is breaking down, as we have already noted. Too late the Vatican has realized the depth of the gulf between the hierarchy and the intelligent layman, and flounders between making conciliatory gestures with one hand and striking an iron fist of orthodoxy on the table with the other. Divisions even within the priesthood are now appearing and the appearance of a breakaway church, claiming its own spiritual authority, is already on the horizon.

The discoveries summarized at the beginning of this book can only bring to a head the disruptive movement already well under way. The Church, and mankind, have reached the end of a road. The historical foundation of the Church lies in ruins, and the moral authority that traced its origin to a myth and a mushroom is no less discredited. But it is not necessarily the end of *the* road. The Church may never recover, at least in the form we have known it, but for mankind generally the break with the past and traditional moral sanctions offers a much-needed opportunity to reappraise our present position and the way ahead. Now, at last, we can stand on our own feet. The props of religion can be thrown aside, the bishops banished from the legislature to their cathedrals and palaces to superintend their fabric funds and tea parties, and we can tackle the problems that confront twentieth-century society in the light of what we want that world to be.

Before us lies the first great hurdle of effective redistribution of the world's riches without violent revolution. It may well be that we shall never pass that point. That could very well be the end of *the* road. But if we fail there, it will not be because we lacked piety, or irreverently laid bare the hoax on which the Church had built its mighty edifice of belief; it will be because we had not had time to throw off the chains that have bound our thinking for two thousand years. We had too long looked for guidance to heaven and the hierarchy, and new problems confronted us which would not yield to the old solutions. The days of the Church's soup kitchens and Lady Bountiful's periodic visits of mercy to the deserving poor of the village were past. The swelling, hungry masses of the African and Asian continents broke out of their insufficient lands and we had no answer but to contain them by force or try to buy them off with charity given too little and too late.

If we are to face the challenge of the immediate future and thereafter, if successful, to regulate our lives to take the fullest advantages of our new technology, we shall need to combine the optimism of youth with the pragmatism of maturity and the wisdom of old age. Every stage of society will have its own special contribution to make and none can be rejected on grounds of immaturity or colour or creed. The world of the twentieth century cannot afford the divisive influences of religion, any more than it can segregate its populations into classes of privilege on the grounds of skin pigmentation. If there is another road opening up beyond this one's end, it is a wide one. The emergent nations will demand to walk abreast of the leaders, who in turn will expect them to share the duties and obligations of responsible hegemony. We have all to graduate quickly into high school and university, but some have to reach those grades in one step from the kindergarten. Perhaps the patience and tolerance that are required from the more mature nations in the world's council chambers will come easier if we have learnt to value the freshness of approach demonstrated by the best of our young people. We may deplore their brashness and have physically to restrain their too easy resort to violence, but in many ways their impatience with the past and willingness to seek new paths to self-fulfilment is a reflection on our present situation. They have sensed the truth that we have reached the end of one road and are seeking another. If they seem too often to be dashing madly in all directions at once, and are more intent on provoking chaos than constructing a new framework for society, they are at least trying to stand on their own feet. The emergent nations are in the same parlous position. They reject the old orders with the shackles of imperialism, and have not yet discovered new moral sanctions to discipline their political freedom. Growing up is a painful process, but if the world survives to adulthood, the new road that stretches ahead promises far greater opportunities for the fulfilment of man's spiritual potential than could any of the old religions. At least he will be able to call his world his own.